D0898262

THE FUTURE

BELONGS TO THOSE WHO DARE

Choosing Your Life
through Strategic Futuring

PRISCILLA ROSE

FOREWORD BY RAYMOND ROOD

The Future Belongs to Those Who Dare
Choosing Your Life through Strategic Futuring
by Priscilla Rose © 2016 by The Genysys Group

Print ISBN: 978-0-99749-540-9
eBook ISBN: 978-0-99749-541-6

Published by

For more information, contact:
TheGenysysGroup.com

First Printing
Printed in the United States of America

This book is dedicated to those brave individuals who have dared to pick up the "Golden Feathers" presented in their lives. They are choosing their futures and by that action, inspire others to do the same. I believe the world needs more people that are willing to take this leap to live future-driven lives, and I welcome the opportunity to support this powerful movement.

This book is also dedicated to six co-conspirators who picked up the Golden Feather of this Genysys story and have endured the many challenges of working with Ray and me to get the Strategic Futuring process out into the world. A special note of deep gratitude to Amy Hoppock and Ilene Bezjian—two people in the Genysys universe that have seen that this book *needs* to be written and have supported this project, including writing initial drafts of several pieces of this book! I could not be more grateful. Four other co-conspirators that had a profound impact on our ability to get Strategic Futuring to this point are Julie Wood, Kristie Haskell, Karen Brightly, and Laurie Reinhart. Our work together brought the importance of Strategic Futuring to the surface. I have been inspired by your personal Strategic Futuring journeys and your desire to see this process become available to others so their lives can be changed as ours have been. This book is for you!

CONTENTS

The future belongs
to those who dare to
envision the future,
treat their vision as fact,
and take responsibility
for translating their
vision into reality.

Raymond Rood
Founder of The Genysys Group

FOREWORD

The Golden Feather Story: The Choice and the Warning
Raymond Rood

You'll notice that the book cover bears the image of a Golden Feather. Many years ago, I was introduced to an iteration of a story based on a Russian fairy tale[1] that I have repeated numerous times in different settings over the years. In fact, I have told it so often that it has taken on a life of its own, with new meanings emerging for both the listener and myself almost every time I tell it. For a number of reasons, I now have come to a deeper understanding of why Priscilla has asked me to write a foreword to *The Future Belongs to Those Who Dare*, and in so doing, tell the story of the Golden Feather as I have understood it, as a way of introducing the symbolic role that the story plays in what you will be reading and experiencing.

In one way, the story is about a choice—a choice that could change a person's life in significant ways, and maybe even forever. In another way, it is about a warning, a warning to proceed with caution. The story is about both opportunities and challenges that emerge from this choice, in addition to support that can come from unexpected sources, often hidden in plain sight if we are not on the lookout for them.

The story has five main characters (the king, the hunter, the horse, the feather, and the princess), each having symbolic meaning, especially as the reader's life journey interacts with the content of this book.

So here is the story of the Golden Feather that has evolved over the years which, as with many old stories, begins with . . .

There once lived a king who had a faithful hunter. This hunter would ride the land on the king's business. The hunter rode a grand, talking horse that was not only swift and strong, but was wise beyond knowing. One day the hunter was riding through the deep forest, when an unrecognizable, colorful blur whooshed across his path, and the forest went oddly silent around him. With the sounds of nature—wind in the trees, birds singing, insects buzzing—forests are rarely truly silent. He realized this must have been the firebird. The firebird was said to be the pinnacle of creation, a large bird of extraordinary beauty and mystery.

In the blink of an eye, she had come and gone, but in the path of the noiseless forest lay a Golden Feather from the glorious bird.

The hunter dismounted and went to retrieve the feather. His horse broke the silence and said, "Do not pick up the feather before you, unless you want to know fear and trouble in your life." But the hunter was determined to deliver the feather to his king, so he gently picked up the feather and rode back to court.

The king was amazed at the gift from his loyal hunter and showered him with gold, silver, and prestige. Then he realized that the hunter could bring him something even more valuable. "Since you have managed to bring back a feather of the legendary firebird, surely you can acquire the bird itself!"

The shocked hunter replied, "Your Majesty, how can I capture a bird that has never been seen?"

The king would not be dissuaded. "You will bring me the firebird or as surely as I live, my sword will pass under your arm and out of your head and you will die."

Knowing that it was useless to argue with the king, the hunter departed, having not an inkling of how to accomplish this request. His horse finally spoke again, "Be not afraid. I will help you find the firebird, but this is not the fear and trouble of which I spoke."

After many toiling journeys and adventures, the hunter and his horse triumphantly returned with the firebird. The king was overjoyed and again bestowed the hunter with riches and even greater prestige. Yet, the king was still not satisfied.

"Hunter, I am a king who needs a bride. Go and bring me back the fair Princess Andromeda, who sails the oceans on a great ship that men know not where."

Dismayed, the hunter protested, "Your Majesty, how can I bring Princess Andromeda to you when no one knows whereupon she sails?"

But his protests only brought more threats of death from the king. Knowing that he could not avoid this assignment, he set forth to find the princess. His faithful horse helped him, but again warned him of the fear and trouble ahead.

Miraculously and with much effort and peril, they returned to the king with his bride-to-be. Still more money and rewards were bestowed upon the hunter, but his journeys were not over. The princess insisted that she could not be married until the hunter fetched her wedding dress, which lay in a casket under 300 fathoms of water.

Again, he set upon his mission blindly and with the assistance and cautioning of his trusty horse. When they returned with the dress, he was greeted with the usual fanfare and gifts. Yet now it was the princess who was unsatisfied. "Your Majesty, on such an occasion there should be an appropriate sacrifice. I demand the life of the hunter."

The king concurred and commanded the castle servants to fill a huge cauldron with water where the hunter would be boiled as a sacrifice. Finally the hunter realized how precarious his situation was and his horse spoke once again. "This is the trouble and fear of which I spoke. Yet, please trust me and jump to the center of the cauldron before you are thrown in. If you follow my instruction, you will be transformed and the water will have no power to destroy you."

With no other choice, the hunter made a mighty leap into the center of the cauldron, and he was transformed. Unmarked by the heat, he deftly swam to the edge and climbed out. Upon seeing this phenomenon, the king declared, "Surely if a hunter is capable of such a feat, then a king can escape the boiling water as well."

The king leapt into the boiling water and sank like a stone. After his death, he was buried outside of the castle. The hunter and the princess were married and they lived a long and happy life together.

The moral of the story is this: In life, there are Golden Feathers scattered at intervals on your journey. To pass by the feather without picking it up is to continue to live life as it is without change. Yet, if you stoop down to pick up the feather, you open yourself to transformation. The cost of transformation is trouble and fear—they are inseparable companions. The choice remains: ignore the Golden Feathers you see and live safely without change, or accept fear and trouble as the price of transformation when grasping at those Golden Feathers.

The Future Belongs to Those Who Dare is about a sequence of stories of transformation and what has been learned by those of us who, when confronted with Golden Feathers, decided to pick them up and not drop them in spite of the fear and trouble they brought our way. In some way, I believe that I have been a Golden Feather for Priscilla, as she and this book may become to you—which in turn you may become to others down the road.

In conclusion, being one who continues to travel this road, I do have one piece of advice. If you choose to read further and decide to travel the path of Strategic Futuring, then be on the lookout for a wise and truthful horse!

Raymond Rood
2016

INTRODUCTION

On the last day of my graduate course, "Leaders as Agents of Change," I walked into class and saw a bright yellow feather on each desk.

Professor Rood started off this final class by letting us know we were now part of a long lineage of rule breakers that lived with the radical notion that our primary job, no matter what position (formal or informal), was to lead our lives—and that to lead our lives was to be fully ourselves. He said that to be fully ourselves, we could not simply follow the rules of others, but had to create our own. That was inherently the definition of a leader.

As he told us the Golden Feather story, in typical Ray Rood fashion, he challenged us to pick up the Golden Feather that represented leading our lives. He declared that we could never claim to be a victim, since we now knew of the option always available to us—to take responsibility for our lives. That is, if we dared!

He closed class with this phrase that encapsulates the essence of this book: **"The future belongs to those who dare . . . to envi-**

sion the future, treat their vision as fact, and take responsibility for translating their vision into reality!"

Over the years, Ray has been a mentor to me of the most powerful kind. I did something completely out of character by reaching out to him for his help after that fateful day in class. Knowing I was in a business graduate program, my brother-in-law asked me to help his company with some challenges he was facing. Since I did not feel at all confident in what I could do on my own, I reached out to Ray on his behalf. I knew from class that Ray had helped many organizations, and I wanted to get my brother-in-law the help he needed. As I saw how my brother-in-law picked up the Golden Feather of *his own way of leading*, I was completely taken aback that it made such a difference.

All organizational change is first personal. I remember reading this in the book, Deep Change by Robert Quinn, that Ray had me read as a part of my work with my brother-in-law. It affirms that all organizations and individuals are heading in one of two directions—slow death or deep change. To choose to do nothing is actually a choice for slow death, since in the fast-paced world we live in, simply maintaining is actually a choice toward decline.

Once he saw his way clearly, we had only to help my brother-in-law make his leadership style functional in his company, which was a departure from the way his father had led the company. He wanted to go a different direction, and his major question was how to make that happen. Like any significant change for an organization, it began at the personal level. The significant impact of this shift even affected the bottom line for the company.

It was such a profound experience—to witness a change of that magnitude—that I knew I wanted to keep doing this kind of work.

As I continued working with other clients and with Ray, he took me through a step-by-step process that clarified my understanding about my own life—the process of Strategic Futuring—which I am excited to share with you in this book. It helped me *see* a life where I had picked up the Golden Feather of choosing to lead my life, rather than letting it just happen and falling victim to the slow death syndrome Quinn described.

In my vision, which I will share in more detail in a later chapter, I was running a company that helped others learn to choose the direction of their lives. As I described my vision to Ray, I told him quite matter-of-factly that I was pretty sure I was running *his* company in *my* future. Although this took him by surprise, he went along with it. It went from an inside joke to reality, as I took responsibility for translating that seed of a vision into something real. This journey has helped me to see myself as "real" and influential—starting with how I choose to live, instead of feeling like life is happening to me, which was how I felt for the first three decades of my life.

In this book, I share with you the journey I have taken with Ray as my guide, along a road less traveled. Much of what I have learned comes from things Ray has shared with me, that gives language to what I've experienced or answers the deep questions I have wondered about. He has expressed his gratitude to me for the many crazy questions I asked along the way, since many times it is only as he shares in response that he understands more of what he has learned in his life.

I also have the privilege to introduce you to a cast of characters I have met along this road, who have also chosen the path of *most* resistance, since as Ray aptly says, *"Resistance and struggle is what forges authenticity.*" Ray has introduced me to these incredible people and I have learned so much from their stories.

Ray's own authenticity gives people permission to live more authentically. As he said in class, living authentically is the true measure of leadership and is the only way we can contribute our best in any setting we encounter.

His response tormented me. If authenticity was so important, why didn't more people choose to live this way? Ray said most people simply do not know this is an option for them. They have no role models, and it is scary to truly live by your own rules and not be bound by others' rules. To be authentic is to live by your own rules, but most people have learned to play it safe. Playing it safe is to live by what others tell you or be who others expect you to be. This resonated with me, especially the hesitation to truly live my life by my own rules and not care what others think or say.

Ray had a role model to follow. He told me the story of how his grandfather took him out of school when he was about eleven years old and told him, "Son, not everything you learn is taught in the classroom." His grandfather was like the wise horse and showed Ray he didn't have to play by the rules. In fact, as Ray learned, if you are bound by the rules, you can't truly be who you are. You live under the tyranny of the "oughts" and the "shoulds."[1]

This perception of what should happen or who you should be becomes a jail of sorts and holds us hostage, even when no one is watching. It's similar to how the philosopher Michel Foucault used the metaphor of Bentham's jail system, the Panopticon,[2] to aptly describe people's fear that everyone was watching them. Bentham had determined his jail was so efficient that it only needed one person to stand guard in the middle of the prison. The prisoners would hold themselves imprisoned by the thought of everyone watching them instead of needing to have multiple armed guards. Sadly, this may be how you feel—it is too dangerous to go outside your cell and incur the wrath of others.

Ray found out much later in life what his grandfather truly meant about not playing by others' rules. After a painful experience, when he was told he wasn't living up to what others expected of him, he said he finally gave himself permission to simply be himself. He thought he was in a cage, but he realized he had assumed the cage door was locked. That was not the case. The door was closed, but not locked. He pushed on it that day, and it opened. That day he was free. He was free to be himself.

I want you to know that by reading this book, you are joining the ranks of rule breakers that now span the globe. They are people that simply refuse to be bound by the confines of what is easy, familiar, and what others say is best. They look inward to seek the answers that are already inside, waiting to be discovered. By picking up this book, you have begun your journey to recognize and pick up the ultimate Golden Feather—leading your life. In Ray's words, **"To lead your life is to be yourself without apology."** Like the hunter, this is the journey of a lifetime, with many quests along the way. The quests are opportunities to learn even more so what it is to be your authentic self, and therefore make your greatest contribution. Remember, you are not alone. There is a tribe of co-conspirators. To conspire simply means to "breathe together." I invite you to join this conspiracy, if you dare. As you make this choice, you will indeed know fear and trouble like you've never known before. It is also the only way to experience the kind of transformation that forges authenticity and allows for the joy of truly being free.

THE STRATEGIC FUTURING PROCESS

The Strategic Futuring process was created and developed by Ray Rood over the past twenty-five years, while working with graduate students, organizational and community leaders, and individuals involved in life transitions. Strategic Futuring is based on sociological research, human development principles, adult learning theories, and organizational transformation experience.

The Strategic Futuring process begins with the following assumptions:

1. Your life is a story only you can tell.

2. Your story begins at birth and you live your story one day at a time.

3. Along the way, you are presented with challenges, opportunities, threats, and choices in every stage of the life cycle.

4. By looking at the past and assessing the present, you can begin to identify a chosen future.

One of the best-kept secrets is that each person has the ability to influence the future to the extent that you

- Envision your future

- Treat your vision as fact

- Plan for its realization

The Strategic Futuring process involves five steps:

Step 1: *Choose* to own your story

Step 2: Dare to ask the big questions

Step 3: See and speak your vision

Step 4: Create your Action Plan

Step 5: Partner for success

The Future Belongs to Those Who Dare helps smart, talented individuals who may feel they are sleepwalking through their lives to become more in charge of their lives, including doing work that challenges, engages, and excites them. They are responsible and reliable but may feel stuck—held back by life's circumstances, and literally unable to see a future beyond the next few months. The process frees them so that they can see a future that excites them and finally feels possible—within their grasp—and so they can step into a life where they have more purpose.

The vision component of Strategic Futuring makes it distinct from other life-planning processes. Many people understand that setting goals is an important part of achieving what you really want, but there are several steps before goal setting that are crucial to give you the intrinsic motivation to set those goals and then follow through on them. They need to be rooted in things you care about rather than what someone says will bring you success. They are much more effective if you can see the life that goal enables, so it is part of a larger picture, instead of standing on its own without context or purpose.

The word strategic tends to have a more business or corporate connotation, but I have learned that the future you want to envision cannot be open-ended, or it loses its power. It must be strategic, which means it must be built on the foundation of who you are, what you care about most, and what you want to know most about the future. I will explore this in a later chapter on envisioning.

HOW TO GET THE MOST OUT OF THIS BOOK

The book you are holding today introduces and explains the Strategic Futuring process. The ideas are valuable on their own, but have **added power when facilitated by a certified Strategic Futuring coach**. It can also be helpful to work through the exercises on your own, and then share them with a friend, mentor, or colleague. A certified coach provides individualized guidance, and you will get the most out of your Strategic Futuring process when you have a coach to encourage you, listen to your story, and ask probing questions to help you see clearly on your journey. Because it is not always feasible to have a coach, I have described this process so it can also function as a self-guided process.

To learn more about Strategic Futuring, see the special section at the end of this book that gives more detail. For now, follow the chapters of the book as your guide.

1

PICKING UP THE GOLDEN FEATHER OF YOUR LIFE

Freedom, by definition, is people realizing that they are their own leaders.

—Diane Nash, Civil Rights Activist

Most of us have had a wake-up call moment—one of those times where you realize you need to make a change. It can come in the form of a medical diagnosis, a relationship breakup or breakdown, a brush with death for yourself or a loved one, or an unanticipated opportunity that forces a good hard look at reality. One of my most profound wake-up call moments happened when I was standing on a chilly station platform in Boston, waiting for the train. As the train rushed into the station I felt myself lean forward ever so slightly and then sharply rock back on my heels. Just inches forward at the right moment and I wouldn't have to survive in the nothingness that I was living in—watching my life whiz by as fast as that train. In that moment, I realized being passive in my life was slowly draining away my desire to live. Without being actively engaged and taking the lead in my own life, I felt trapped, with no way out.

The moment on the train platform was shortly after I had started working with Ray, and I was beginning to "wake up" to how unconsciously I had been living. For most of my life, I knew very definitely that I was not in charge. On any given weekend, it could be 3:00 a.m. and my five siblings and I would still be putting up drywall. My dad directed his makeshift army to keep focused on projects like the basement remodel in our house in upstate New York. I was tired but didn't dare ask to leave the project. As was the case on most Saturdays, we were in project mode and things like sleep were a luxury for the post-project era. To stay off the radar, I was a good soldier and did what was required. This was the beginning of living my life unconsciously.

Even as I grew up and experienced my first few mind-numbing jobs, I continued to do what I was told, and it was effective in making my bosses happy and making money. **However, life seemed to be happening *to* me.** I felt like a bystander to my life—watching it go by and wondering where it would take me. I went off to college because that was the next logical step, if I didn't want to keep doing the same jobs. I got another job at college to pay the bills and pay for school. After seven years of doing the next thing that came across my desk, I was in middle management and still plugging away blindly. This all seemed normal to me; I never thought there was another option.

Passively floating from job to job, following orders, and following the script I thought was written for me led me to that place on the train platform where nothing seemed to matter. Ironically, I didn't care enough to purposely lean forward. I didn't care enough about stopping the pain to end my life, but I didn't want to live either. I began to realize that living passively wasn't really living. I wasn't "showing up" in my life. Like the hunter, there was a point when I took charge of my life. Shortly after the moment on the train platform, Ray offered the Strategic Futuring process as a Golden Feather—and I knew I needed to pick it up. The alternative was not working. The Strategic Futuring process awoke the possibility of a life beyond just surviving from one day to the next. Later, I learned this passive way of living was the "reactive" approach to life (one of the Four Approaches, to be explained below).

As you begin to understand the primary ways you approach people and situations in your life, you will become more aware of how the logical end of your actions impacts the future. You can then decide if your current approach will move you forward or if it is holding you back. This puts you in charge, and you can then decide how to proceed, rather than acting without thought. A key to this process is being intentional about your choices and considering the cumulative results of your approach down the road. Is your primary approach sustainable over time? Ask yourself, how would you *prefer* to approach your life?

The Golden Feather represents a choice that could change your approach to your life and create the possibility of a better future. You may see glimpses of possible futures as you reach down to pick up the feather. Even with the warnings about the fear and trouble ahead, you see this as a worthwhile risk. When the hunter picked up that feather, he took charge of his life in a new way. This wasn't on his list of orders for the day or in his job description as a hunter. He was going off-script and felt compelled to pick it up.

Why does taking charge and taking greater responsibility in life matter? Without taking charge, it is like being a passenger in a car and being taken for a ride. Even though there is much you cannot control that comes into your lane of life, wouldn't you rather be in the driver's seat and holding onto the wheel? That is what it is to pick up the Golden Feather of taking charge of your whole life. To be truly free is to be in charge and leading your life, as Diane Nash expresses so eloquently in the opening quote to this chapter.

Have you had a Golden Feather moment, when you knew you had to make a major change in your life—you needed to choose your own way?

The first part of the Strategic Futuring process that Ray shared with me was recognizing the different ways to show up, be visible, and make decisions that impact the future. Often the first or reflexive way is simply reacting, as I had been when I was blindly moving from job to job to pay the bills. How are you showing up? If you can see and assess how you are currently approaching your life, it can also help you see an option other than just surviving.

INSTRUCTIONS: EVALUATE YOUR APPROACHES TO YOUR FUTURE

Consider how you make decisions, and fill in your estimates using the exercise on the following pages.

Step 1: Reflect on the questions and then allocate a percentage of time you feel you spend in each approach. Do you see yourself spending a majority of your time using one of these approaches? Do you find yourself in a reactive mode, just surviving and "putting out fires"? Do you take time to pause when you have a decision to make (responsive)? Are you thinking ahead and proactively much of the time, or do you fixate on the future and inventing your life?

However you conclude that your response modes are currently allocated, the four areas should add up to one hundred percent at the bottom of column two in the exercise on the following page.

Step 2: Identify how you would prefer to spend your time. After you have completed the assessment of how you currently respond in column two, move to column three. The four lines represent the same four approaches, but instead of being your current mode of operation, they represent how you would rather spend your time. The four areas should also add up to one hundred percent at the bottom of the column.

Your desired percentages may be quite different from your present allocation of time (your current reality). Give yourself some time to work through the exercise.

FOUR APPROACHES TO THE FUTURE EXERCISE

The Four Approaches	Current Reality	Desired Reality
Reactive Approach (Survival): Reacting to the immediate future through direct, unconscious, intuitive action. The driver = the situation	_____%	_____%
Responsive Approach (Creativity): Responding to the emerging future through pausing to consider as many alternative approaches as possible before taking action. The driver = the problem	_____%	_____%
Proactive Approach (Opportunity): Anticipating the future through identifying emerging trends and projecting their outcomes into the future. The driver = the opportunity	_____%	_____%
Inventive Approach (Vision): Creating the future by envisioning what is possible, including its pathway, and utilizing the resulting vision as a guide for planning. The driver = the imagination of individuals	_____%	_____%
TOTAL PERCENTAGE OF TIME	_____%	_____%

JOHN'S STORY
THE HIGH COST OF LETTING SOMEONE ELSE DRIVE

In the same way that I felt about my life that day on the train platform, John J. Perry had come to a crossroads: he had to take back his life or risk losing it. I first became aware of John's incredible story when Ray recommended I use one of his assessments to look at how my poor alignment in my job was draining my energy and causing physical symptoms similar to what John described.

In his first career, John worked as an aeronautical research engineer at the NASA Flight Research Center. He was privileged to work with Neil Armstrong and many other esteemed colleagues in the early years when space exploration was a highly visible and exciting new frontier. He was energized by his work, and the culture within NASA at the time supported creativity and innovation, and allowed people to make mistakes—once.

Long after the moon landing, he had worked his way up the ladder into a role where he managed and documented how the center spent taxpayer dollars. He took this role very seriously and was still engaged in his work, primarily because his supervisor trusted him to do the job the way he operated best. Then, things shifted dramatically for John. He was a few years from retiring with full benefits when his new boss changed all the rules. He was not to communicate with any other upper-level management, and before he talked with anyone above his pay grade, the communication had to be approved by his new boss. John was also pressured to reimburse this boss for his personal expenses, which John was not willing to do.

Every day this new supervisor checked in on John, essentially breathing down his neck and watching his every move. He did not operate well under this pressure and was filled with anxiety whenever he saw his supervisor coming up the stairs to the main building entrance. He had headaches every day and could not sleep more than a few hours each night. He awoke each day dreading what the day would hold for him. Within eighteen months, he was on stress leave and his doctor told him if things didn't change, the stress he was experiencing would likely have serious health consequences.

John Perry resigned from his job, choosing to leave NASA within three years of retirement, because he cared about his health and his future, and he refused to gamble with his survival for the time it would have taken to get to his long-awaited retirement.

After leaving this job, as John healed, he poured himself into studying why this new supervisor had such an impact on him. At the time, he wondered if he was the only one—but came to see that there were many people who, like he had been, were in serious pain as a result of their workplace environment. He realized his job functions had stayed the same, but the behavioral expectations had changed dramatically.

As a result of his studies, he developed an assessment tool called the Job Person Environment Assessment, that helps individuals assess their behavioral preferences in a job and the behavioral expectations of a job, and then matches them to see where potential challenges and opportunities might be. It also looks at how supportive the environment of an organization is—according to the employees—and identifies what can be improved to make the organization more supportive for its employees. That assessment is still in use today, and John Perry was able to move in a new direction in his career as a result of its development.

John J. Perry has now helped thousands of individuals to see how they can create better tomorrows for themselves by understanding how their work experience boosts their energy or drains it.

CAPTURE YOUR LEARNING

At the end of this and each chapter that follows, take ten minutes to capture your learning. This is an important step in making the new information applicable to your life. Don't limit yourself on this step.

To help prompt you in identifying your most significant learning, reflect on these questions:

- Was anything surprising?

- Was anything new?

- Was there anything you already knew that was reinforced in a new way?

- Did any themes emerge?

What have you learned from exploring how you are currently approaching the future and how you desire to approach your future?

What Golden Feathers are showing up in your life?

CONCLUDING THOUGHTS

Choosing to take charge, to take an active role and lead your life, is the first step in making your best contribution. For me, as I realized how much I was just reacting to my circumstances and understood what that was creating in my life, I knew I needed to make a change. I didn't know exactly how to do that, but passively letting life happen to me was not a viable option.

People often spend sixty to seventy percent of their time in the reactive/responsive mode and would prefer to shift to spending the majority of their time using the more strategic approaches (proactive/inventive). This can impact and shape the points when the reactive and responsive approaches may be needed.

In the next step of the Strategic Futuring process, I will help you see that you already have much more practice at picking up Golden Feathers than you might have thought. You can powerfully access your past successes as you then look to define the future.

THIS ISN'T YOUR FIRST GOLDEN FEATHER

I saw the angel in the marble and
carved until I set him free.

—Attributed to Michelangelo

I was recently with a group of women who have experienced things many of us did not know were possible for humans to endure. And yet, they were sitting in front of me and I was in complete awe of these women, who I considered to be modern-day heroes. They had chosen their own lives, at great risk, well before they went through Strategic Futuring. I realized that by going through Strategic Futuring, they began to understand their heroic stories at a deeper level.

The process showed them the value of continuing to choose their lives and therefore choose their futures, instead of feeling victimized by what others expected of them. After going through Strategic Futuring, one woman, who had literally been held hostage by her husband, in seclusion from her family and friends, shared what she had discovered through the process. She said she needed to continue to do what *she* knew was right for her and her children, instead of what others mandated for her. She needed to continue to lay claim on her own life. Then, she could be truly free. She had made the scary choice to leap out of that situation or risk that she literally may not be alive the next day.

When you make decisions like this, although perhaps not as dramatic as the above example, you are choosing to play by your own rules. As you work through the Strategic Futuring process, you will gain clarity about your story and will begin to feel more comfortable in your own skin. In many ways, this can help your skin to thicken so you are less impacted when others say or do things that could derail you.

At the end of the fairy tale, the hunter jumped into the cauldron and yet he was untouched by the boiling water that threatened to consume him. However, he had been through so much as a result of picking up the Golden Feather that he became immune to the heat that would have quickly taken over a mere mortal, as it did the king. By embarking on the quests, he had become superhuman and was untouched by those things that would normally have brought someone to their demise. This transformation, by embarking on quest after quest, was what made the hunter a hero in the end.

HERO STORIES UNCOVERED

I always wanted to have a "comeback" story—a hero's story of sorts. The one where the hero chooses the road less traveled, overcomes adversity, and ends up stronger on the other side—and able to help more people as a result. I felt if you had a comeback story, then you had a purpose for being here. Because I didn't have a good story, I felt my life was somewhat meaningless and it held no real purpose. I was just taking up oxygen.

What I began to uncover, as Ray walked me through Strategic Futuring, was that I had been taking more risks than I was aware, including even asking Ray to meet with me. This was not something I would have done in the past—approaching an authority figure and asking them for their time. How could I presume that I was worth the time? I did not want to be a bother or waste their time. However, for my brother-in-law's sake, I continued to meet with Ray, despite the fact that it was not easy. It was out of my comfort zone, since I had been used to hiding in the back of the classroom (as Ray described) behind a desk, or behind the safety and semi-anonymity provided by being at the other end of a telephone line. Although I was not aware at the time what I was choosing, I wanted to make a greater contribution, starting with my brother-in-law, and so I embarked on what Ray later shared was the "hero's journey." Joseph Campbell said a hero is simply "someone who has given his or her life to something bigger than oneself." You may not know how you want to contribute, until you look at your story and see what has been driving you and what is worth taking the risky "road less traveled."

Robert Quinn, in his book *Deep Change*,[1] also references the "hero's journey" as a critical component of any significant change. The hero starts out as an average person in their ordinary world. Then something happens and they're given a call to action (i.e., a Golden Feather presents itself). They accept the challenge, face their fear, and in the process the hero dies a metaphorical death, only to be reborn in some new way. In the end, the hero returns to the ordinary world—transformed and untouchable by certain forces that may have taken them down prior to transformation—and is able to use this superpower for good.

AUTHENTICITY = RESPONSIBILITY

What you know about your past story, including the joys and also how you have navigated challenges, gives you important clues about what is important to you, what you are willing to take risks for, and the strength of character you have uniquely developed from your quests/experiences.

Discovering your own authenticity is the ongoing process of uncovering and owning who you are and what you are going to do with who you are. At the bottom line, it is discovering and owning your purpose. This is at the heart of the Strategic Futuring process. It is the belief that knowing your story of the past and what makes you unique is at the core of seeing how you can make your best contribution in the future. It is not creating something from nothing, but it is as Michelangelo said, "Every block of stone has a statue inside it and it is the task of the sculptor to discover it."

As Ray shared in the graduate course I took, "Leaders as Agents of Change," in many ways it is the major task in your life, should you choose, to discover the statue that is already inside you—the angel that longs to be free. It is when you are free that you are most authentic. Consequently, it is when you are authentic and choosing to live your purpose that you are most free, instead of unknowingly imprisoned by the rules/expectations of others. You have the opportunity to be an active co-creator of your life, instead of a passive receiver or victim.

What is so dangerous about those that see or have seen themselves as victims to their lives is that, in many ways, they are always looking for a "savior." They are looking for someone else to blame for where they find themselves, and without taking full responsibility for their lives, they are constantly looking for someone or something to rescue them. You can see this in the plethora of reality-altering substances available to those who seek to avoid their reality and sense of responsibility. It is also easy to point out those people who need to put responsibility anywhere but on themselves. However, it is more difficult to see when you are the one playing that blame game. I know this well.

As Ray shared with my class, it is only from the place of leading/owning our lives that we can make our best contribution. This is our ultimate goal—the ultimate Golden Feather is owning who we are and our responsibility to be ourselves "without apology."

The great news is you are not starting from scratch. The challenges—the quests brought on by the Golden Feathers—are what allow you to uncover what is hidden.

You may not think of yourself as the hero in your story, like the hunter in the fairy tale, but a hero is simply one that risks the safety of the familiar, ventures into the unknown, and overcomes the challenges in their path to ensure a brighter future. I'll bet you can name times just this week when you have done something that was a bit risky or dangerous. You're reading this book, so add that to your list! This is not the first Golden Feather you have picked up in your life, and it will not be the last. You are more of a hero than you might think. You may not even be aware of the brave choices you have made, especially the choices to do things differently than others may desire, differently than what is expected, differently than you have done in the past, or differently than has been modeled.

The important thing about your story is to know why you are taking the risks. What about your story makes the risks worth the fear and trouble you will find? I see few people that know their story well. And yet, I find the most powerful people are those that know their stories and can readily reference key high points or low points and decision points in their lives, including why those decisions were important to them at that time. They know what they learned from the quests/challenges they faced. They can tell you how they chose to allow it to make them stronger. They can tell you how the strength allowed them to contribute more fully.

TYPES OF DISCOVERY

One type of discovery—to uncover who you are—is imagining your future, as you will do in the visioning exercises later in the book. Once you have seen the future you want to have, an audacious next step is verbalizing your story and purpose to other people (as you will do in the sharing and feedback exercises that follow visioning). However, you cannot really own this vision until you put your intention into action in the public arena. This builds emotional muscle and clarity, and comfort in your own skin. Building your authenticity is a process that happens over time. As you are authentic in real life, you recognize it in yourself, and so will other people. Everyone begins their life as an unconsciously authentic child. A four-year-old child acts totally as themselves, without apology. As you get older, you learn how to follow other people's rules and to conform to societal norms. In social settings, you are asked to conform. If we as a society didn't have social norms, there would be chaos—but in many ways, a major part of adulthood is calling into question the norms and rules, and choosing those that you deem will serve you in your future. If you don't do this, you end up living as you were acculturated in your past, through your upbringing. Erikson[2] outlined how this interaction with societal norms pushes each person to determine their identity.

Ray shared how he came to recognize this developmental pathway in his own story. When he was in high school and his family was moving, he realized that he didn't like how he was living his life. He felt that he was living someone else's life—mostly the life his parents wanted for him. For example, he was dating a girl and his grandfather asked him why he was dating her. He responded that his parents liked her. His grandfather told Ray it would be good for his parents if he broke up with her. Ray did break up with her before he moved, and he decided that in the new school he was going to be different. He said at first he felt as if he was making it up, but he kept discovering and rediscovering what was more natural to him. He decided not to let his natural tendencies be overly

45

dominant. He chose what he wanted, and eventually that started to feel more natural.

Ray risked feeling that he was making things up, but what he felt was at risk was his own life. He chose to be uncomfortable for a while, instead of living someone else's life. When you understand your story and why you take risks, you can risk even more—on purpose. You know what cause you are serving. You are creating the possibility of a better future.

YOUR FOUNDATION

Each of the exercises in this chapter will help you get to know your own story. They will help you think about the story of what brought you to the particular place you are now. Keep in mind the types of situations in which you have been willing to take risks. Why were those risks worthwhile? What experiences have brought you to a fork in the road or a Golden Feather moment?

To reconstruct the foundation, accomplishments, and purpose of your life, the following exercises in order will walk you through a natural progression to bring clarity to your understanding of who you are.

1. Lifeline

2. Accomplishments

3. Strengths and Challenges

4. Values

5. Mission and Purpose

We all live in a fast-paced world that barely allows the space and opportunity to reflect, let alone consider the purpose and reason for existence. You may feel you cannot afford to take the time. I would argue you cannot afford *not* to take the time. This reflection is the foundation upon which you put all of your other efforts.

There are now over seven billion people in the world, and the world population is estimated to grow by seventy-five million per year, hitting eight billion by the year 2030. Even among all those people, there is no other person that holds exactly the same values, life experiences, and strengths as you. Your unique perspective has been forged by this combination. You can see most clearly through your lens when you allow yourself to be fully your authentic self. You'll find those places where you feel most naturally and completely yourself and also the most alive. You are not trying to be someone else, or the version of you that you feel is acceptable or that someone else expects. The world needs your authenticity—in some way it is calling for it. Frederick Buechner said that your calling is that place "where your deep gladness and the world's deep hunger meet." It is my hope that you will come to appreciate the importance of your story. Understanding what makes you unique is the foundation for the entire Strategic Futuring process. Strategic Futuring is not about creating something from nothing; rather, it begins with clarifying the primary elements of what makes you, you. Only after this step can you consider your future. The following reflective exercises will help you clarify who you are so that you can begin to see yourself as a hero, and that being a hero is someone whose life and story is more valuable as it becomes a gift to be given away. The hunter had become very valuable, because of the journey he had taken and his contributions because of the risks he chose to take.

INSTRUCTIONS: LOOK AT YOUR LIFELINE

Plotting your life will give you a visual of the peak experiences of your life as well as the challenges or "valleys." As you reflect on this, you can begin to see the choices you have made.

The hunter may have plotted his birth and some highs and lows of coming up through the ranks to become the king's valued huntsman. There may have been times he was successful and times he came close to losing his status. He may have dealt with any number of realities with his family—births of siblings, marriages, or the death of a parent.

On the excercise that follows, you will see a line with a zero on the left side and a question mark on the right side. These two symbols represent the beginning of your life and some point in the future when your life will end. It is not a practice in anything other than to visually display the length of a typical life and what could possibly occur. Each line will be different, as each person lives a unique life.

Step 1: On the lifeline, draw a vertical line where you think your current age should be.

Step 2: Working back toward the zero, place vertical lines at the ages representing both positive and negative occurrences in your life. This could include the birth of a sibling, graduations, and accomplishing new skills—as well as divorce, deaths, or perhaps an unfortunate event that led to a lifestyle change.

For the positive events, list a word or two above the horizontal line and for the negative events, list them beneath the line. Use the space beneath to explain the events and how you have used them or learned from them since their occurrence.

Two things arise from this exercise. First, events have affected your life and helped you to continue on and work toward positive outcomes. Second, there have been setbacks from which you have survived and maybe thrived.

We are each a combination of our past life events, and in the Accomplishments exercise following the Lifeline exercise, you will begin to plan for the future by examining all the experiences from which you have learned. Fill in your lifeline below and then draw a continuous line moving from one event to another.

LIFELINE EXERCISE

0  ?

ACCOMPLISHMENTS

Don't ask yourself what the world needs. Ask what makes you come alive, and go do it. Because what the world needs is people who have come alive.

—Howard Thurman

When the hunter brought the Golden Feather to the king, it might have been one of his most significant achievements to date. He chose to enter the woods, risking danger, and had recognized an opportunity that others may not have seen. Achievements are those moments, days, and experiences in life when you feel joy, fulfillment, and a sense of being "alive." You may sense that you have made an important contribution to your family, friends, job, local community, or even a broader impact. They can be significant events or small moments of delight. Many times we are so immersed in living our lives, day to day, that we don't feel we have time to stop and reflect on those times, experiences, and places in life when we have felt most satisfied, or fully alive.

INSTRUCTIONS: IDENTIFYING ACCOMPLISHMENTS

Think about those times in your life that satisfied you, when you felt good about what you were doing. If you struggle to quickly identify those events, don't rush. Most important are those actions or qualities that represent how you want to see yourself, what you do well, or what you want to be known for.

Step 1: Using the following exercise page, briefly describe the first three to five moments/days/experiences that come to mind that are meaningful or left you with a sense of satisfaction.

For example, I put completing my master's degree program as one of my most satisfying achievements.

Step 2: Go deeper. As you identify those moments or experiences, pay special attention to the verbs you choose. What were you *doing* when you felt proud and most alive? Make sure the verb you identify is the action that made you feel fully engaged.

As I thought about what I was *doing while working toward my master's degree*, I realized it was that really it was *persevering* through every challenging assignment, even though at each turn I wanted to quit. Even then, I couldn't see how it was serving my future, so I questioned why I was even putting in the effort, when I was working full-time and had many other responsibilities with my family at the time.

Step 3: As you think about those moments, look for the common themes running through them. These moments are the times when your values, beliefs, and passions all lined up and you felt great. These can be large or small things. Capture those things that first come to mind.

Perseverance was a theme for me, since all of the things I felt most proud of had required sticking with them, despite significant challenges. This can often be a theme for others as well.

ACCOMPLISHMENTS EXERCISE

What are your three to five most significant achievements or accomplishments?

1.

2.

3.

4.

5.

What themes do you see in these stories?

STRENGTHS AND CHALLENGES

Greatness lies, not in being strong,
but in the right using of strength . . .

—Henry Ward Beecher

If the hunter had done an assessment of his strengths and challenges, perhaps he would have seen other times while becoming a hunter when his courage and risk-taking had served as strengths and also as challenges, by getting him into situations he didn't necessarily know how to navigate at the outset.

Now it is time to explore your strengths and challenges as a part of uncovering your story. These are characteristics, like the hunter's courage, that you utilize as you go about your life and work, and navigate your relationships. The more you are aware of your strengths, the more you can embrace them. Donald Clifton and Marcus Buckingham affirm in their book *Now, Discover Your Strengths*[3] that the most successful individuals are those that not only are aware of their strengths but find ways to live and work mostly within their strengths, while still managing their challenges. Their research showed that most people give more energy to attempting to change themselves and their weaknesses, instead of living more fully in their natural strengths. Clifton and Buckingham's book has an assessment test which identifies your top five strengths. It is worth your time and money to get the book and take the assessment. This book is listed in the Resources section at YourDaringFuture.com.

INSTRUCTIONS: IDENTIFY YOUR STRENGTHS AND CHALLENGES

Some strengths may be obvious to you, but some are not. Knowing your strengths can confirm choices you have made in the past and guide you in future decisions. Likewise, understanding what skills and circumstances are challenging for you can help you choose successful paths and identify opportunities to work on your challenges. Follow these steps to identify your unique combination of strengths and also your challenges.

Step 1: In the following exercise, identify your strengths. Strengths can include qualities, actions, thought processes, or relational skills you do well and that bring you energy. They are the things people might ask you to do because they know you excel at performing them.

For example, one of your strengths might be organization. Go deeper, though, to see if you like organizing people, or tasks, or both—and why. What's a good story that speaks to this strength?

Step 2: Next, identify your challenges. Challenges can include qualities, actions, patterns of relating, and habits you feel are ineffective or not necessarily helpful in your life. These are things that consistently do not work well and may inhibit your ability to be successful in some areas of your life. As an example, a challenge may be that you like to control every aspect of events, including vacations where that may not serve you in relaxing or when it may frustrate family members.

Step 3: Go deeper. After you articulate both your strengths and challenges, go back and prioritize the ones you see as your top strength and top challenge. This helps you explore which aspects of your personality you utilize most. It's akin to knowing if you are right-handed or left-handed, and can help you be aware of what you favor.

Step 4: Explore the relationship. What do you see as the relationship between your strengths and challenges? As you look at these together with a coach or friend, you may see that your challenges are the "shadow" side of your strengths. Taking the time to explore the relationship helps you to solidify them even more and enables you to leverage them.

In the examples above, the challenge of overplanning or controlling events can be the shadow side of being very organized and really enjoying organization. The more you are aware of this, the more you can embrace the strength and also know how to manage the challenge associated with that strength. You can gain help from others in doing so as well, to help you stay in your positive energy.

STRENGTHS AND
CHALLENGES EXERCISE

What would you consider your top five strengths?

1.

2.

3.

4.

5.

What would you consider your top five challenges?

1.

2.

3.

4.

5.

What relationship do you see between your strengths and challenges?

INSTRUCTIONS: VALUES

*It's not hard to make decisions once you
know what your values are.*

—Roy E. Disney

Values are defined as the beliefs that guide you in carrying out
your mission and purpose. It's important to identify these and also
clarify what each value looks like in action. Many times, we think
we value something until we compare it to what we are actually
doing in our everyday actions. When you take time to really think
about and understand your unique values, you understand how to
use and apply them better.

Step 1: Using the following exercise, identify your values. Ask
yourself what happened in your life that helped you to see each
as a value. What is the story? When considering your values,
it's tempting to write what you should value; instead, reflect on
what you really value. For example, you may say, "I value honesty," yet, if you lie to your children and tell them, "McDonald's
is closed today," do you value honesty more, or peace? This is
an opportunity to reflect on some difficult questions. Be open
to learning about yourself and what you really *do* value. Your
story around each will help illuminate this.

Step 2: Prioritize your values. Our values are constantly in com-
petition with each other so this is very important to see which
value "trumps" the others. For example, the hunter may have

thought that he valued keeping himself safe so he could provide for his family and serve the king, but then one could argue that he valued creating a better life in the future more and was willing to risk his life for that possible future.

Step 3: Identify how you know you are living out this value. This includes what this looks like in everyday actions, like the McDonald's example above. What was one way you lived this out this week? This will help you gain specificity around something that might seem abstract.

These steps involved in connecting with your values are designed to help you build the foundation for your hero's journey. We all live by values—a certain "code"—but many times these values have not been defined, and it could be argued that what is not reflected upon is misunderstood. We don't have to go as far as Socrates in saying it is not worth living, but it is critical to do this reflection.

You may have also had "wake-up calls" along the way that called out an inconsistency in your values. This happened to me recently with a colleague who knew that I talk about my value for relationships. When a conflict came up, I wrote an email instead of talking to them in person and they perceived this to be inconsistent with my value for relationships. This was difficult for me to hear, but I was glad I had articulated my value and had the opportunity to see what that really meant in this specific situation.

VALUES EXERCISE

What are your top five values? (List them in prioritized order.)

1.

2.

3.

4.

5.

For each of your top five values, describe how you see this value reflected in your everyday life, or in choices you have made.

1.

2.

3.

4.

5.

INSTRUCTIONS: PURPOSE AND MISSION

The place God calls you to is the place where your deep gladness and the world's deep hunger meet.

—Frederick Buechner

Here is how purpose, mission, and values relate:

Purpose: This is the context or reason for your life—your *why*

Mission: The expressed outcomes of your purpose—*what* you are here to do

Values: The beliefs that guide you as you carry out your mission

Don't spend too much time on this initially—just write what first comes to mind. The most important thing at this time is to take a first pass at articulating your purpose. Naturally, this will be an ongoing exploration throughout your life. You will continue to gain clarity over time, but you need a place to start.

Step 1: Identify your purpose. Purpose can be viewed as your talents merged with your passions. For example, things that seemingly have "chosen you" rather than you choosing them. It's like you are "called" and the calling is hard to avoid.

Why are you here? What unique "need" are you impassioned to address throughout your life? A colleague described your purpose related to the one question you are here to answer. She said there was a boy that, even as a kid, kept asking his mother, "What's under the ocean? What's under the ocean?" He became the father of plate tectonics.

Do you believe you have a unique purpose in life? What is the very first thing that comes to mind when asked about your purpose? What is your story behind what you see as your purpose?

For example: If you were born with the gift of music, one of your purposes may be to utilize that gift. Your mission would likely be the outcome. Will you sing, compose, conduct, or teach? If you were born with the gift of organization, perhaps your mission could be in the field of business, psychology, or education.

Step 2: Articulate your mission. Mission is more a question of the outcome of your purpose. It is more *what* you are here to do than who you are. Your purpose is the context or reason for life; mission is how your purpose is expressed. Take a first pass at articulating your mission, even if you're not sure it's right. There is no pressure to get it perfect.

PURPOSE AND MISSION EXERCISE

What do you understand to be your life's purpose and mission?

(Mission is *what* I am here to do; purpose is *why*—the need I am fulfilling through my mission.)

Mission:

Purpose:

EILEEN'S STORY
UNCOVERING THE VALUE OF VALUES

From the moment I met Eileen, I sensed that she had a powerful story. I learned that Eileen was faced with a reality in her health that shifted her perspective on her life. As she went through Strategic Futuring, the values she always had came into focus in a new way and allowed her to take a big step forward into a more daring future.

Eileen and I met at a leadership workshop where I shared my journey of feeling that my life was a series of reactions I had little control over. When I found Strategic Futuring, I learned a way to come alive by owning my life and my story and following my vision of helping others do the same.

After the workshop, Eileen approached me and told me that my story resonated with her and she would really like to meet and hear more. I shared more of the details of my journey and the role that Ray and Strategic Futuring played, and this brave woman shared *her* story with me. I was blown away.

Eileen was twenty-five and full of energy and ambition as a young professional, pursuing a master's degree. Eileen explained, "I was always taught how important it was to work hard and be successful." As she was going about her normal routine on a normal day, she noticed she was losing vision in her left eye. When she realized this was not getting better, she went to the doctor. After going through a series of tests, Eileen was diagnosed with Relapsing-Remitting Multiple Sclerosis (RRMS), which can cause parts of the body to fail without warning. Most of the time these losses resolve after treatment, but need immediate attention—as Eileen found out that day.

Eileen's diagnosis necessarily called into question a great many things, ranging from logistics of treatment schedules, to finances, to the deeper questions about what this meant for the present and the future. Eileen realized during this time what an amazing support system she had and how important her family, her faith, her friends, and her local community were to her. She leaned into them as she saw both the challenges and the gift of her diagnosis.

Eileen and I met several years after her diagnosis. When I suggested that I take her through Strategic Futuring, she was hesitant. Naturally, she was especially unsure about looking fifteen years into the future, and she was candid in sharing that she simply did not know what the future held. Eileen preferred things that she could control and what she had learned was "the only thing predictable about MS is that it is not predictable." I was impressed that Eileen pushed past this very real unknown and trusted me—and trusted the process. We did get to look at her future, but *first* she came to better understand her values. She affirmed her values and commitment to her family, her faith, her friends, and her community. One value that came more clearly into view was her value for allowing her life to make a difference in the lives of others, even beyond her local community. She knew this had always been a passion of hers and she was consistently asked to contribute in highly visible ways—whether it was being asked to sing at major celebrations, representing her city in a pageant, acting as a master of ceremonies for countless events, or officiating weddings. This list goes on.

As she grew more and more rooted in her values and the stories that illustrated those times that had been most meaningful, this prepared her to look forward. When Eileen did the vision work, what she saw surprised her. At the same time, it felt realistic, feasible, and consistent with previous big dreams that she had before some of life's circumstances had planted some seeds of doubt. Most notably, Eileen saw a life where she was traveling, speaking, writing, and inspiring people from a place of authenticity and grounding in her story. She was relieved to see a future reality where she was flourishing physically, spiritually, and relationally. Eileen had a family of her own and continued to invest in her parents, immediate family and friends, and community as well. Eileen was also excited to see the career she had built—speaking, writing, and sharing her story to inspire young women struggling with chronic illness.

Eileen began to see how much of herself she had sacrificed by "playing it safe" and choosing the security of what was known and familiar, while closing down some of the possibilities of living in the fullness of who she saw herself to be. While her diagnosis naturally brought a sense of loneliness and hopelessness at times, she also described how it allowed her freedom to change and create a new and more expansive vision for her life.

"Strategic Futuring allowed me to use my energy to examine my values and move forward rather than becoming overwhelmed. I gained tools to take action and see possibilities. I realized my dreams are everywhere—all low-hanging fruit."

There is a connection between quality of life and hope. Eileen anchored her soul in her faith and learned to trust herself more fully. She created her own rules. She allowed herself to be more loving toward herself and in her relationships. She has a hunger to grow and learn, exploring and witnessing wonderful surprises that grow out of hidden places.

CAPTURE YOUR LEARNING

At each leg of our hero's journey, we need to "find the hidden treasure." It's at this point that we pause for reflection. What have you learned thus far? Too often in life, you don't take the time to think about what you have learned, and how that new information can be best used. As you take a few moments to pause and say, "What did I learn from this?" you are doing several things:

Identifying the most significant learning about yourself:

- Was anything surprising?

- Was anything new?

- Was there anything you already knew that was reinforced in a new way?

- Did any themes emerge?

Don't shortchange yourself by skipping this step at the end of each session! As I worked through the process, some of my biggest aha moments came as a result of taking a few minutes to say, "Now, what did I learn from the process today?"

By the simple act of naming and describing it, you make it usable and transferable into your everyday life.

CONCLUDING THOUGHTS

As you gain greater clarity about your foundation, the form within the rock starts to become more visible. The Golden Feathers you have already picked up in your life may have appeared ordinary, but hopefully they now have greater significance in the context of your story. You may begin to see your own hero's journey emerging from your choices to create and follow your own rules.

In the next chapter, you will explore how your questions become a powerful framework for looking to the future.

3

DARE TO ASK THE BIG QUESTIONS

My interest is in the future because
I am going to spend the rest of my life there.

—Charles Kettering

One of the most powerful questions I have heard in my life came at me like a freight train from Ray. At the time, I was a manager at a university. I had a lot to say about what was *not* going well. From my perspective, students were getting misinformation, deadlines were unrealistic, and policies were being ignored. I was in charge of making the final decisions about who walked in the graduation ceremonies. It was the culminating moment of all the students' efforts, so there was sometimes a lot riding on my decisions. There were several policies related to this that I did not create, but had to enforce. People at the top overturned my decisions consistently. Faculty went to bat for students, sometimes without considering the ramifications beyond graduation day (i.e., a large percentage of those students that were allowed to walk "short" never finished their degrees, which was why the policy was created). At the height of frustration one day, I was expressing to my mentor, Ray, everything that seemed to be conspiring against me and how "they" just didn't get what they were doing.

Ray responded by asking, **"What are you going to do about it?"** That was the freight train.

My initial reaction was to respond emphatically with, "Nothing! There's nothing I can do." I was thoroughly, completely, and utterly annoyed by the question. I felt if he had been listening, he would have understood that these issues were clearly outside my control. I reflected on that question while I drove home that night, at dinner, and the next day as I walked back into the office. His question kept coming back to me. The possibility of something other than my small reality began to emerge. I felt myself walking a little taller, seeing myself as a little more powerful and a little less a pawn in someone else's chess game. The power of this question still reverberates with me today. It literally brought me to life. And now, I use this question to torture countless other people— and bring them possibility.

I learned from Ray that we already have all the answers we need. The missing piece is that we often do not have anyone asking us good questions or helping us articulate the really important questions that emerge from challenges or experiences. On our hero's journey, in order to look forward to any future, we must uncover the questions that are most important to us. In addition, how we frame the questions either opens or closes down possibility.

Questions also hold inherent assumptions. For example, I recall working on a Strategic Futuring exercise for the first time to articulate the greatest questions I had about my future. One of my questions was, "Will I contribute anything of significance to my world?" At the time, I really did not see myself as contributing anything significant, even though I did want this. The second time I did the exercise, my assumptions about myself had changed and my new question was, "*How* will I contribute significantly to my world (my immediate community and the larger global community)?" Even this small nuance felt completely different to me. By then, I was different.

I help others now on the front end to begin shifting assumptions immediately, knowing they are creating their future, even just by the kinds of questions they ask to achieve more awareness and open the door for possibility and vision.

Some questions can feel more like one you would ask of a Magic 8 Ball. Do you remember those? "Will I be happy?" Responses: Yes. No. Maybe. Looks likely. Doesn't look likely.

Asking different questions will lead to more powerful and significant responses as you then look forward to the future that lets your imagination play. The final piece in creating the foundation for your vision involves identifying some of the biggest questions you have about your future. This helps you make the shift from looking at the past to orienting toward the future.

WHY THINK FIFTEEN YEARS AHEAD?

When I work with clients during Strategic Futuring exercises, I usually invite them to imagine fifteen years in the future. Fifteen years is a set time in the future, chosen strategically, because it is far enough in the future that it pushes you beyond what you know so you "turn on" your imagination, yet it is not so far into the future that you have no sense of reality.

Most planning work doesn't go far enough into the future. When you stay within five years, your imagination is limited by two things:

- First, you are limited by what you know is possible; i.e., you know too much of what will happen inside of five years! It does not stretch your imaginary muscle. It's like when you are lifting weights using too little weight—your muscles really don't warm up. For example, if you already know you only get two weeks off for vacation each year, it would limit you from imagining yourself in a job that doesn't even have specific time off.

- Second, you are limited by your sense of responsibility for what you see. If you automatically see that you are responsible to make what you see happen, it limits you. If you envision something "too big," it can create fear that you only have five years to make it happen. For example, with organizations I find people are reluctant to raise their hands to share what they see is possible because then the boss is likely to say, "Oh, that's a great idea! Why don't you take the lead to make that happen?"

It is not until you move beyond a sense of predictability and responsibility that the freedom to envision exists.

INSTRUCTIONS: YOUR FIVE GREATEST QUESTIONS

One of the hunter's greatest questions could have been, "Will I still be a hunter in fifteen years or will I be doing something else to serve the kingdom?" Perhaps he had asked his horse this question on one of those long rides in the woods, or his horse had dared to question him about what he really wanted.

Your next exercise is to identify your Five Greatest Questions as you look ahead fifteen years. We all have questions about the future, yet sometimes speaking or writing out those questions can be intimidating. If you could have a glimpse of what is to come, what questions would you want answered?

For me, posing questions about my desired future brought about even more thoughts. In line at the grocery story, in the shower, in the coffee shop working on other things—it became surprisingly easy to think about all the questions I really had about my future.

Step 1: List all of your questions about your future. Or you could start with themes and write a question for each theme in your life.

Some themes might be

- Professional: What type of activities will I be involved in? What will I be doing for work? Will it be something I enjoy?

- Relational: What relationships will be important? Will I have someone in my life who loves and cares about me? Will I have a family?

- Purpose: Will I be doing something of significance for my community/world?

- Physical: How will I value my body? Where will I be living?

- Spiritual: How will I be growing?

- Financial: How will I support those I love and myself? Will I be financially solvent? Will I have enough not to worry about money? Will this happen before I am retirement age?

- Intellectual: How will I be challenging myself to continue learning?

Step 2: Group like questions together and see if there is a "bigger" question that encompasses smaller questions.

Think about the things that matter to you and capture those thoughts. How will the world be changing, and will you change with it? What could you imagine if there were no barriers or constraints? Now is the time to get curious and ask your horse all the big questions.

FIVE GREATEST QUESTIONS EXERCISE

Keep in mind what you learned about your unique purpose, mission, values, and achievements from those exercises in the previous chapter as you answer these questions.

From what you know about yourself today, what are your Five Greatest Questions as you look forward to fifteen years from now? Fifteen years from today will be: _____(year).

1.

2.

3.

4.

5.

Review your Five Greatest Questions and determine if there is a theme. If so, write the themes below.

WAYNE'S STORY
QUESTIONS THAT MAKE THE DIFFERENCE

I met Wayne Herron through two mutual colleagues—of course, one colleague was Ray. When I met Wayne, he was literally glowing as he told me about the vital role that Strategic Futuring had played in his coming to trust himself again and seek out a job where he could make his best contribution. He was so effusive about the process that I just had to find out more. I have learned I enjoy finding Wayne venues to share about his story as well, because he communicates it so well and loves sharing his story with others so they can find what he has found.

Wayne had worked in a series of jobs and had come to a crossroads as he approached the age of fifty. His former two positions had been incredibly challenging and draining. He was losing hope that he could find a job where he could thrive in an organization that was more in line with his values, particularly his value for nurturing people while carrying out the day-to-day business. This had been sorely missing from his last positions. He needed to be in a role where his "wings were fully extended and he was permitted to fly." He described that he felt his wings were clipped in many of the positions he had held previously.

There was a six-month time period when he was between jobs that was highly transformative for Wayne. It was during that time that he met with Ray, and Ray brought him through Strategic Futuring. Wayne was a highly reflective person by nature and was asking the haunting question of "Who am I and why do I exist?" as a young man, when he made a decision to come to faith in high school. Even at such a young age, Wayne knew he wanted to be used by God to make a difference in the world. He lived by St. Francis' admonition to "preach at all times and when necessary use words." He wanted his life to be a reflection of his faith. He wanted his behavior to make the impact, not necessarily his words. Ray helped him dig deeper around this big question, given his commitment to find an organization whose mission and vision matched his own personal values. He wanted to be free to help people unlock their potential. He carries his top five strengths on a card in his wallet; his top strength is "Developer." Through the process, he came to understand that he needed to be in a role where he was allowed to help people succeed and exercise his value for developing people. After this time of intentional reflection and seeking, he found a position at Dignity Health, where their top value is dignity and they operate with the value that everyone matters. The company shares his core commitment for people.

Wayne has stated, "Now I am the most content, fulfilled, satisfied, and at-peace professionally that I have ever been in my twenty-year career in philanthropy. I give credit to this process for helping me uncover what was already there."

For Wayne, there was something new that he discovered about himself in every session. He recalled Ray particularly challenged him during him vision work to write how he wanted his tombstone to read. He said, "It is simple—but I believe powerful: 'He loved God, he loved people, he loved himself.' I have grown in all three areas—and I suspect will continue to until my days on earth are over."

Wayne exudes a magnetism that I believe comes from this deep understanding of himself and comfort in his own skin, that he says was profoundly strengthened by going through Strategic Futuring—to embrace his values and strengths to an even greater extent and to envision a life and career where he was living authentically. With this clarity as ammunition, he went after what he really wanted and now supports others to find that same freedom.

CAPTURE YOUR LEARNING

Taking the time to capture your learning is an important step in making the information you have been learning applicable to your life. Take ten minutes to answer the question below.

What is your greatest discovery in describing who you are, where you find yourself today, and your Five Greatest Questions about the future?

Again, in identifying the most significant learning, the questions to reflect upon are:

- Was anything surprising?

- Was anything new?

- Was there anything you already knew that was reinforced in a new way?

- Did any themes emerge?

CONCLUDING THOUGHTS

Like Wayne, reflecting on the big questions creates possibility. It creates the context to look to the future. You may not be able to see beyond what is currently happening. What you do see is often more of the same. Looking forward must be grounded by the firm foundation of who you are and framed by the questions that matter most to you so that it is not too open-ended. This makes your "futuring" truly strategic. My hope is that through the exercises in these first three chapters, you are creating openings to the future and beginning to see cracks of light coming through.

In the next chapter, it is time to use your imagination to see the possibilities that come from picking up your Golden Feather.

SEEING GOLDEN FEATHER POTENTIAL

*The only thing worse than being blind is
having sight, but no vision.*

—Helen Keller

As the hunter reached down to pick up the Golden Feather, it was the idea of what was possible that made him pick it up. However faint it may have been, it was an initial vision or foresight of what could happen that he was picking up. It was hope for a better tomorrow. There was fear in the trouble that lay ahead, but also excitement about the options and potential that would not be possible otherwise.

In this next part of the Strategic Futuring process, you will also get a glimpse of what could be possible from picking up the Golden Feather of your life. Below is a description of part of my fifteen-year vision. I originally envisioned a Wednesday and then expanded to an entire week. This is what my Monday looked like.

Monday I wake up and eagerly look out my window to take in the view of the expansive ocean just beyond the tree line. A new day is here; what will it bring? Clark is still trying to catch a few more Zs. I feel the soft carpet beneath my feet as I emerge from my bed. I tiptoe downstairs, grab some tea, and make for the porch and my favorite chair. I journal a bit and sit for a time to find my center before I start the week. After hearing commotion in the kitchen, I take a deep breath and shift to join Clark and my youngest, Drew, for a quick breakfast of eggs and fruit. Then, they are off to work/school and I take my place at my desk. I bring up my calendar that spans the whole wall using a tiny projector that is my home office system. I love seeing my calendar for the week so large and organized in vibrant blues and greens.

After I get a visual of my week, I start to prepare. There are a class facilitation, several client calls and meetings to prepare for, two new client meetings this week, Genysys Affiliate partnering conversations, the bi-monthly meeting with Genysys leadership, one donor conversation, and an Institute meeting with a partner and the Board. In between everything, I am always working on ideas for my next book and developing ideas to continue the dialogue on the voice-o-sphere (which is just a voice version of a blog).

At 11 a.m., I make a call to my "partner in crime"—aka Genysys COO—and we chat briefly, confirm goals for the week in relation to Genysys, and confirm what we'll need to cover at the weekly leadership meeting on Thursday. This is an exciting time for Genysys in the wake of our twenty-year anniversary celebration last year! I gave a speech describing our journey of the last twenty years and our significant accomplishments, including our international recognition as the world's leading consultancy! Although some people there had never met Ray or known about his vision forty years ago, it was a day of great significance. I am preparing a TEDTalk describing this journey and sharing how others can create and live their visions the way Ray did. I am so glad he got to see the fruit of his intentionality and investment into many lives, including mine! I presented the vision for the next twenty years of Genysys as we expand our movement, full of energy for what lies ahead!

I take a break for lunch.

Perhaps you are like me and never felt like you had much imagination. I watched as many of my friends pursued their dreams of making an impact by becoming lawyers or nurses or psychologists—but I did not have those dreams. Like many, I could not see a future beyond the next couple of months. I just saw more of the same. I saw my job was to make other people's lives work. I dragged myself out of bed, whispering under my breath, "Please don't make me go to work today." I was living for the paycheck, living for those two federally mandated fifteen-minute breaks, living for happy hour after work to numb out the day, living for weekends and vacations to recover from work. Looking back, I wonder if this was really living. I was surviving. And this all seemed normal.

As I went through the envisioning exercise you'll find at the end of this chapter, I was utterly shocked that I could see so much. After firmly rooting myself in my story of the past and my core identity (as you've now done through the exercises in the book thus far), I then journeyed through the visioning exercise.

As you can see in the excerpt at the opening of this chapter, I used my imagination to walk through the day, from the time I opened my eyes in the morning until my head hit the pillow at night, fifteen years in the future. I saw a life that was very different from what I had been experiencing in my present. What surprised me most was that I was quite different—not physically, but my way of being. As I walked by a mirror on this day, I saw myself and I was calm and confident, yet playful; I had routines in place that were physically healthy and others that nurtured my soul. I was running a consulting company and loving it. I was teaching via hologram and loving how the technology allowed me to expand my ability to work with people worldwide. I was working with an amazing team and the work I was doing was meaningful and life-giving, as opposed to life-depleting. The interactions I saw with my spouse and my kids were light and fun, but also productive. At the end of the day, as I went to sleep that night, I reflected on how grateful I was for such a full and good life.

I believed that what I saw might just be possible. It felt so real. It was different from the present, but not out of reach. The moment I considered that this might be possible, I started to feel more alive. My vision gave me hope that something else was possible.

THE VISIONARY MUSCLE

Children are masters of the skills of imagination and envisioning. Next time you have the opportunity to watch children at play in their envisioned world, watch closely and appreciate what they can teach you. Imagine two children playing—they are on a ship, and one is the captain and the other the trusted shipmate. They are on an adventure to rescue animals from the savage pirates on the high seas. There is no doubt in their minds that what they see is real, and they treat it as such as long as they are in the mode of play. And yet as adults, this visionary "muscle," for many of us, seems to have atrophied. As in our physical bodies, if we do not exercise our muscles regularly, they atrophy quite quickly.

As preparation for the exercises of envisioning you will work through in this section, take a minute to recall one of your favorite childhood memories. Mine was playing in the sandbox with my three sisters behind our house in upstate NY. It was a hot, muggy afternoon and we decided we needed to cool off with the hose. The water was so refreshing as we put our hands out to capture that coveted coolness. As it flowed to our feet, we dug our toes into the sand like we were at the beach. We quickly grabbed up the clumps of sand that were becoming saturated and shoved them down each other's backs, seeing the awe of surprise turn to glee. It became quite a mess (sorry, Mom), but it was a rare moment of pure play.

As you do this exercise for yourself, feel the air; smell the smells; feel the joy, excitement, and anticipation. Use your imagination as if you were four years old again. Remember the people there with you, including any imaginary friends who nobody besides you ever met or saw.

This short exercise is a great way to get your imagination muscle working. As you have grown older and taken on the cares and opportunities of the adult world, you may have lost that magical and critical skill of envisioning.

Visioning is not uncommon. You can pick up any book, from those by Stephen Covey to Deepak Choprah, and they encourage you to have a vision. The challenge is that you may not find good instructions on *how* to vision, especially if visioning is new to you and/or you haven't exercised this muscle in a long time.

Envisioning is the active process of using your imagination and playing with possibilities. The actual vision is what you come up with as a part of the experience. It is best to write it down and capture it.

People do vision boards as a different way to capture what you see and experience. This is a great thing to do as well. As you approach visioning here, you'll notice a distinct style that is different from other methods. Sometimes it is helpful to do all of these, since each may help you access a different part of your imaginary muscle— similarly to how you would do different physical exercises to get at very specific muscles, each doing a unique and necessary job.

Almost all people experience something that is useful by going through the exercises. It may not be a full vision, but even feelings, smells, images, or the lack of images can be helpful information. Whatever you see, it is data for you to use as you move forward. It is not an end in and of itself. A vision is never an end, so please release yourself from feeling there is a right way to do this.

How you interpret what you experience is a critical next step.

THE APPROACH TO VISIONING

This approach to visioning

1. First **grounds you in reality** and who you are—clear stories, themes, and questions as an opening to possibilities.

2. Then **guides you into the future**, using a formula that works to unlock and exercise your imagination.

The skill and tool that makes up the Strategic Futuring version of envisioning was adapted from the work of sociologist Elise Boulding[1] from Dartmouth College. Ray heard Elise Boulding speak at a conference in Boston in 1982 about the power of vision. Boulding, having been deeply impacted by wars that kept her from being able to go back to her native home of Norway, became a leader in the peace movement, and her major research question grew from this perspective. Over her thirty-year career, her major question was, "Why do groups of people either stay together over time or dissipate?" She found two principles that operated in both groups—those that stayed together and those that dissipated.

Groups that stayed together:

1. Had a picture or vision of themselves thriving together in the future; and

2. Treated this vision as fact and not just hope

They didn't know how it would happen, but they used the vision as a way to decide what to say yes or no to. The vision became the grid or filter for all the daily decisions. When challenging circumstances happened (which was inevitable), they got curious about how that would serve the vision.

Groups that dissipated followed the same two principles:

1. Their picture of their future together was no picture (they did not see themselves together or thriving).

2. They treated that picture (or rather lack thereof) as fact.

When challenges arose, they assumed, "Well, I didn't think it would work out anyhow," so they allowed circumstances to pull them apart, because they did not have anything keeping them together.

Elise Boulding and her husband, Kenneth, utilized their research in work with the United Nations to help envision a world without nuclear weapons. Influenced by the work of Dutch scholar Fred Polak, they hosted workshops in the 80s with diverse groups of people who shared an interest and passion for a world without nuclear weapons. Boulding's years of research and experience had taught her that **if we cannot *see* what peace looks like, we cannot achieve it.**

The Bouldings were influenced by a theory called "level-of-aspiration study." The idea was that how individuals expect they will perform in a future situation is predictive of their actual performance. They came to believe that to have a picture of a desired future is empowering in the present.

A vision of the future seems to have a magnetic power to draw us into the future and, just by having it, we start creating more of our future and are able to be proactive, instead of just reacting!

The skill and tool of envisioning gives our adult minds permission and freedom to dream, tapping into our deepest desires and play that we accessed so easily as children.

Things to keep in mind when envisioning:

In this part of the process, you will walk through a day fifteen years in the future. As you walk through this day, you will be uncovering and revealing things that you already know, even though you may not be conscious that you know them. The assumption that you know more than you are aware of is part of this approach. Just go along with it and see what emerges for you.

You will work a muscle that has not been exercised for a while, for most people, so it may be uncomfortable or not what you expected, but remember it is just an exercise. There is no pressure for a particular result.

Regardless of how fuzzy the future feels, you are still developing the muscle just by utilizing this exercise. If you do it again after a month, or if you try it facilitated by someone else, you may see something else come from it that was not there at first. The first vision exercise I did in graduate school was probably the hardest assignment I ever had to complete—and I was a very good student. We were required to imagine first that we were sixty (or thirty years beyond where we were) and what we had accomplished at age sixty. Honestly, I was tempted to find out where Ray lived, show up at his door, and demand a refund. OK, I'm being dramatic, but I do remember it distinctly, although some interesting things came to my head eventually. I was running a marriage retreat center with my husband. I had a PhD and I had published a book. These were things I didn't even know I might want.

It may be difficult at times, but I encourage you to press on. It is important to simply take note of what comes up and not to place judgment on it. In some ways, similar to dreams, it is most powerful to simply ask what it is saying to us. **Vision is not an end in and of itself, but a doorway to the future.**

The envisioning is not purely open-ended or rhetorical, because you are leveraging what you already know. For example, because you have already defined that, for example, you value relationships and have created a question around how to build stronger relationships, the vision you create is going to be more fully grounded in who you are than if you had not done the exercises.

So, if you have not completed the exercises in the previous chapters, be sure you do this first! That is what makes it strategic; your vision will speak to things you are really interested in finding out.

If you know that these kinds of exercises are a challenge for you, you may want to have a friend facilitate it for you (see the facilitator's notes below). You can also download the guided audio version that is available online at YourDaringFuture.com. Your mind may need a little more help as you exercise this underutilized muscle, and a facilitator can be incredibly helpful. The verbal prompts help you to move though the exercise, and then you can just notice what comes to mind, instead of needing to think about what comes next.

FIND THE RIGHT ENVIRONMENT

For the following exercises, make sure you are in a comfortable place and have sixty uninterrupted minutes to invest in this envisioning exercise. Setting can be very important. I recommend finding a place that gives you "space," like by the ocean or at a lookout point on a hill or mountain. These actually allow your brain waves to expand so you can think creatively. Even though the exercise may only take fifteen minutes, give yourself the gift of space and perspective on either side of the time as well, so you don't feel rushed to move on to the next thing. This will help free your imagination.

INSTRUCTIONS: VISION PART 1

Step 1: Review your most satisfying accomplishments, strengths and challenges, values, and purpose/mission from those exercises.

Step 2: Review your Five Greatest Questions about your future from that exercise in the previous chapter.

Step 3: Set up your scenario. Fill in your scenario below to get all the details in place. Put in the year it will be, the age you'll be, the ages of significant people in your current world, the exact day and month it will be. Note: we usually use a Wednesday because it captures what is happening on a typical day as opposed to a weekend or a vacation.

Step 4: Review the visioning instructions you will be walking through on the exercises page. Don't write anything down at first. Just get in your mind what you will be doing. When you walk through the exercise, use your imagination as a guide. It usually works best to close your eyes as you do the exercise just to block out any outside distractions. It should only take a few minutes to walk through the exercise. Then when you open your eyes, write down everything that you saw, using the prompts in the exercise.

Step 5: Get comfortable. Close your eyes if this feels comfortable to you. Walk through the visioning exercise of the day fifteen years in the future.

Step 6: Open your eyes. Write down what you saw or felt or experienced, using the prompts on the exercise pages.

Facilitator's note: Facilitators, encourage the person you are facilitating for to get comfortable physically and close their eyes to shut out distractions. Let them know at the end of the exercise, which will be just a few minutes, they will write down what came to mind. Invite them to use all of their senses and let go of any kind of critical judgment about what they experience. Then, simply speak out the prompts in the Vision Exercise Part 1 slowly with a three- to four-second pause in between each statement. Skip the bold headers. Start with, "Waking up on this day, what is the first thing you are aware of?" "Look around. What catches your gaze?" "Is anyone with you?"

When you have spoken out the exercise, remind them to take time to write out what they saw and experienced as they walked through the exercise, using the prompts in the following exercise pages.

VISION EXERCISE PART 1

It's a Wednesday in _____ [current month], _____ [year, fifteen years from now]. Be aware of how old you are. How old will any significant people in your life be (spouse, kids, parents, etc.)?

1. **Waking up (place, location, with whom)**—waking up on this day, what is the first thing you are aware of?

   • Look around. What catches your gaze?

   • Is anyone with you?

   • Get out of bed. What do you feel under your feet as you emerge from bed? Explore this place/your home—what do you find?

   • Take a peek out the window/s if there are windows. What do you notice? Do you note anything about the geography (location)?

2. **Preparation for the day (dress, routine, organization)**— next, observe yourself as you prepare for the day. How do you organize yourself for the day? What's your routine?

   • As you are readying yourself, you might even look in the mirror. What's your image of yourself? What do you see?

   • Who else is a part of your morning routine?

3. **Morning activities (what, where, and with whom)**—move into morning activities. Use that image you saw as you follow yourself through this day. What do you do this morning?

   - Is anyone else a part of your activities?

4. **Lunch (where, with whom, and what takes place)**—it's lunchtime. What do you find yourself doing?

   - Where are you?

   - Who is with you?

5. **Afternoon activities (what, where, and with whom)**—moving into your afternoon activities, what takes place?

   - Are there others around or involved?

6. **Evening (where, with whom, and what takes place)**—evening has come on this day—where do you find yourself?

   - What are you doing?

   - Who is with you?

7. **Going to sleep (reflecting on the state and meaning of life)**—as you go to sleep this night, reflect on your life.

   - How do you feel about this day?

   - How do you feel about your life?

   To download a pdf version of this exercise,
   go to YourDaringFuture.com.

ANSWER YOUR GREATEST QUESTIONS

Take the Five Greatest Questions you articulated in the last chapter, list them again here, and take a few minutes to answer your questions, based on what you envisioned. Play with this—assuming what you envisioned will happen, what would be your responses?

1.

2.

3.

4.

5.

INSTRUCTIONS: VISIONARY MILESTONES

Life can only be understood backwards;
but it must be lived forwards.

—Søren Kierkegaard

Creating a Strategic Futuring vision is a two-part process. The first part is to visualize your future state, which you have just completed. The second part, which is equally important, is to figure out how you arrived there. Strategic Futuring starts with a vision of the future and moves into the present by the identification of *Visionary Milestones*.

Elise Boulding said it is not enough to have a vision. She found in her research that you have to see a pathway. She helped Ray come up with a way to help people create a "visionary pathway," so they could see how they arrived at a certain place by standing in the future and asking another imagination-provoking question: "How did I get here?" So, let your imagination play with that. Answer with "It's a great story—let me tell you about it!"

Step 1: Fill in the blanks in the Vision Exercise Part 2 to orient yourself.

Step 2: Take yourself back to the end of your day in your future reality (fifteen years in the future), right before you go to sleep, as you are reflecting on the fullness and value of your life.

Step 3: When you are in that reflective mode, look back on your life over the last *five years*. Recall the milestones that led you to this point. What events took place, what decisions did you make that contributed to your reality?

Ask yourself, *what actions did I take, five years in the past?* What events/decisions took place? For example, you might say, "I remember now—five years ago in 2025, I made the decision to move overseas."

Step 4: Take fifteen minutes to describe the events and decisions that took place five years ago. What were the pivotal dynamics?

- Write one to two details for each
- Repeat this exercise for
  - ten years ago
  - fifteen years ago
  - twenty years ago (I realize this seems strange to go back five years before this present year, but you are in the middle of your future so you've already been doing things that are contributing to your future!)

VISION EXERCISE PART 2:
VISIONARY MILESTONES

This exercise is designed to link your vision for the future with both the present and past.

Before beginning this exercise, identify the following dates and your age at each date:

Fifteen years from today, the year will be _____; my age will be ___.

Ten years from today, the year will be _____; my age will be___.

Five years from today, the year will be _____; my age will be ___.

Five years ago today, the year was _____; my age was_____.

From the perspective of your 20_____ (date fifteen years from today) reality, it is time to look back in increments of five years and describe what events took place and what decisions were key to the vision you have for your life in fifteen years. Answer using present-tense language.

20____ (ten years from today)
List key decisions or events that helped me get to where I see myself in _____ (date fifteen years in the future).

20____ (five years from today)

List key decisions or events that helped me get to where I see myself in _____ (date fifteen years in the future).

20____ (today's year)

List key decisions or events that helped me get to where I see myself in _____ (date fifteen years in the future).

20____ (five years ago from today)

I achieved the following things (or these key events took place) that helped me get where I see myself in _____ (date fifteen years in the future).

IMPORTANT QUESTIONS TO ANSWER

Don't skip this step! Respond to these thought-provoking questions.

Will any of this happen? What do you feel is the likelihood that what you have envisioned will take place?

What percentage of what you saw in your vision will happen?

_____% will happen.

What will need to happen for your vision to become real?

Elise Boulding would say that what you just envisioned is going to take place if

- You treat your vision as a fact (not just hope).

Raymond Rood would add that what you just envisioned is going to take place if

- You plan for it.

INSTRUCTIONS:
LIFE AREAS/GOAL AREAS

Vision without action is a daydream.
Action without vision is a nightmare.

—Japanese proverb

This exercise helps you come back to reality. You did the visioning exercise and now have an idea of what options are available to you. In order to move toward this vision, you need to see what steps you can begin making now in the direction that you see yourself in the future. Start with three to five areas that, if you focus on these in the next two to three years, will set you on a path toward your vision.

Sometimes it is as simple as investing fifteen minutes a day practicing, learning, or developing relationships or habits that will set you up for success. If you invest fifteen minutes a day every day for a month, you would be spending the equivalent of one workday each month investing in your desired future.

GOALS EXERCISE

In order to move toward your vision, what three big Life Areas (finance, health, career, family, etc.) do you need to focus on doing or developing over the next three to five years?

1.

2.

3.

4.

5.

These are your Goal Areas.

INSTRUCTIONS: VISION STATEMENT

People are capable, at any time in their lives,
of doing what they dream of.

—Paulo Coelho, *The Alchemist*[2]

Now it's time for you to write your Vision Statement. A personal Vision Statement is a powerful tool that will help you make decisions and guide you as you live your daily life.

The hunter's Vision Statement might be something like "I see myself becoming a highly valued member of the kingdom where I am known as the go-to person to call on to overcome seemingly insurmountable obstacles."

The value of a Vision Statement is that it provides you with focus and criteria for decision-making. You are more likely to know what to say "yes" to and even more importantly, what to say "no" to or "not now." A clear and compelling Vision Statement can serve as a filter when sorting through many opportunities and relationships that present themselves on a daily basis.

Step 1: Start writing your own Vision Statement by simply completing the sentence, "I see myself becoming . . ."

Step 2: Post your statement in prominent places (on your bathroom mirror, bulletin board, on a card in your wallet, on your phone's home screen, etc.) as a guide and a daily reminder of the future you envision and are working toward.

A Vision Statement should be:

- **Inspiring**. It is something that makes you excited at the possibilities it holds. Play with it to make it move you!

  - For example, Paul saw himself becoming "the voice of the millennials.

- **Tangible**. It is based in reality and is something you can achieve.

  - For example, if you are afraid of heights, it wouldn't make sense that your Vision Statement included becoming a fighter pilot—unless it also included overcoming that fear.

- **Beyond your present grasp.** This is where you can be. It serves as a challenge to get you to where you know you can be.

  - For example, Kathy's vision included becoming a published author and writing a book about her story.

- **A functional decision-making tool**. A Vision Statement will help you know what opportunities you need to take advantage of, or create in your life, to achieve your vision. Sometimes the good can be the enemy of what is best, and your Vision Statement can help you sort through all your opportunities.

VISION STATEMENT EXERCISE

With this criteria in mind, complete the sentence below. This will become your Vision Statement.

In light of who I am, my vision, and my Visionary Milestones, I see myself becoming . . .

Sample Vision Statements can be found at
YourDaringFuture.com.

PAUL'S STORY

VISION IS ABOUT PLANTING A SEED, NOT CHASING A DREAM

Paul Angone's story illustrated to me how many visions are born—out of the combination of our experiences, particularly pain we have experienced, and skills we have developed in navigating the pain. We also see that we are not alone in experiencing this pain and we "go first," as Paul describes, in putting language to that dynamic and passing on what we have learned in addressing that dynamic. Gaining clarity of vision in describing your goal and then seeing a pathway to that goal is more like planting a seed and finding ways to nurture it and let it grow.

Paul's vision was born out of his own frustration. As he moved from college into the "real world," armed with freshly minted skills and knowledge to make his mark, his excitement turned to dread as he had some less than magical job experiences. These left him disillusioned about what his career was going to amount to and how one truly figured out what to do after the glow of college dimmed and the reality of life sunk in.

He looked around and saw his friends struggling with the same things he was, and they were not talking about it. They were back in their parents' basements, hiding out, depressed, and there was no language or permission to talk about the very real struggles that seemed unique to twenty-somethings, particularly in the millennial generation. He found his friends were suffering with "Obsessive Comparison Disorder," as he coined it—the OCD of his generation, made uniquely possible by the onslaught of social media with all its inherent expectations to display only rainbows and unicorns, but was effectively taking people down into dark places of hiding the truth with no visible way out.

Paul started writing about what he was seeing and experiencing. First it was cathartic, and then he began to see himself as the voice of a misunderstood generation that, like him, did not immediately understand its own strengths and opportunities. As he watered this seed of a vision, he hit roadblock after roadblock. He was rejected by publishers who wouldn't take a risk on a new author. He kept writing. He came up with idea after idea for products that he could sell to create his own business, so he wouldn't have to stay in dead-end jobs. He kept writing. He went to graduate school because surely he just needed to know more about the subject in order to figure out how to make a living doing what he cared about.

It was in graduate school that he met Ray Rood and at the end of class, Ray offered him a Golden Feather. Ray offered anyone the opportunity to meet with him for coffee after the class ended. Paul finally took Ray up on that offer and Ray offered another Golden Feather. He offered to take him through the Strategic Futuring process.

Challenge accepted. Through Strategic Futuring, Paul regrounded himself in what he really cared about and also the strengths he had that prepared him uniquely for what he saw as his calling. He realized that, instead of creating a separate business to pay the bills or waiting for something to break and for someone to take a chance on him and publish his book, he as himself was the business. He had been taking a very traditional approach and it wasn't working.

Soon after one of his blogs went "viral," Paul wrote and published his first book. Then he literally quit his job—to pursue his vision of writing for, speaking to, and inspiring the millennial generation. Paul's success in following his dream was an inspiration to me, since I was developing my own vision journey from within the same company that Paul left, during the same time frame.

When I was interviewing Paul about his story, I asked the question, "If there was one thing you could tell people about doing this vision work, what would you want to tell them?" His response surprised me.

Paul said the vision is more like a seed that you plant, as opposed to a dream to chase. He said so many people are chasing their dream and if they have not tracked it down, they are discouraged. He stated that you plant your dream and nurture it throughout your life.

CAPTURE YOUR LEARNING

It is important to reflect on the personal learning and insights you gain as you work through the concepts presented.

By identifying what you have learned, you can use what you know. Unexamined, unidentified knowledge is unusable knowledge.

How did you approach the envisioning exercise? Did you notice any emotions as you began the exercises (excitement, resistance, fear, anticipation, etc.)?

What was your most significant learning as a result of the visioning exercises in this chapter?

Did the strategic life/goal areas that you identified (the three to five things you need to focus on in the next three to five years) surprise you, or did they make sense?

How did it feel to create your Vision Statement?

CONCLUDING THOUGHTS

If you see it, you can create it!

You've done great work on this! In the beginning, you identified where you find yourself today—you took a snapshot. Now you have a snapshot of a possible future that you can begin to choose. It's not just any future. It is connected with who you are, framed by the questions that are most pressing. If you can see it, you can truly begin to create it for yourself.

When we have a clear and compelling image of what we want life to look like, we do not live out of the past. We can work to create that positive future we envision.

TALK TO YOUR HORSE: SHARING LEADS TO BELIEVING

Isolation is a dream killer.

—Barbara Sher

After I did the envisioning exercise, I shared what I saw with Ray.

I swallowed hard as I realized the gravity of what I had just put out there so casually. I hadn't thought much about the fact that what I was sharing would impact him greatly. It seemed more matter-of-fact, since he had asked me to share what came out of my vision work.

I told him that I saw myself running a company that was similar to the one he founded (and for which I was currently doing some contract work). I told him that I was pretty sure it was **his** company that I was running in my future. There was silence on the other end of the phone and then Ray said, "Oh, really?" It was only then that I heard myself say to an important authority figure in my life that I was going to be running his company. Now, this was a fifteen-year vision, so it's not like it was happening the next week or year, but still! Suddenly I was emboldened by the vision work. And as I saw it, it seemed perfectly feasible and desirable for all parties. I did backtrack quickly and let Ray know that of course, he would have to "buy in" (literally) to this idea since he did own the company (minor detail, right!?). Ray shifted to his mentoring voice and said, "Actually, **you** will have to buy in to the idea first. I'm not sure that you do yet. Then, you will have to enroll me in your vision. Then, you will have to convince everyone else around you that this is a good idea." It was my turn for silence as I took in what he had just said.

As you share your story of the past and of the future with another person, it starts to become more real and not just an idea or a dream. Expressing the idea gives it the best opportunity to move from an idea into something real, because you begin to feel it is possible and you begin to take responsibility for making it real.

Many of us have dreams for what we want in life, but in some ways we are scared to speak them—perhaps for fear they may not become real. What might be possible if you spoke your private vision aloud? Is it possible you can speak something into existence? Something akin to a self-fulfilling prophecy?

After sharing what I saw in my vision work with Ray, I decided I had fifteen years to convince a lot of people, starting with myself, that what I saw was a good idea. I had found a Golden Feather and I picked it up, not knowing the least bit what fear and trouble would await me—and also, what transformation would be possible.

SHARING AND FEEDBACK

Your vision is just a seed, as Paul Angone described. Think of it like that. The next step is to find two to three people in your personal or professional life with whom you feel comfortable sharing your experience so far in this process, including your vision. If the hunter hadn't had the horse to confide in and help him on his journey, his journey may have ended very differently. It was not by accident that the hunter's confidante was a horse, since horses in literature often represent loyalty and stability and even a trusted friend, carrying their rider into battle or on a long journey. People may become your accountability and support partners later in the process. For now, you are choosing them because they know you and you feel safe as you take this significant step to share your vision.

For me, I told three people. I didn't feel that I had a lot of choices, so I chose my mentor, my sister, and my former partner. My vision was a pretty radical departure from my life at the time. In fact, my sister recently told me she really struggled to see what I was describing, especially that *I* was running a company. It was as if I was telling them I was going to fly to the moon. That wasn't the person they recognized.

Find two to three people that hold some of the qualities of the ideal confidante. Share with them your vision for the future, including your milestones and your visionary answers to your Five Greatest Questions. As you talk about your vision of the future, remember to use the present tense. "I am working, I am doing, my family is, etc." This may seem and feel unusual—however, it is an important exercise because it will help to cement in your mind the probability of your desired future, which, as we have established, will make the achievement of your desired future more probable.

Keep in mind you might not get the response you want. The hunter did not get the response he was probably hoping for. Instead he was warned about the fear and trouble ahead. Even a reaction you're not expecting may add fuel to your vision, like it did for the hunter and it certainly did for me when I told Ray what I saw.

When stating your Visionary Milestones, standing in the future vision, those milestones have already occurred so be sure and use past-tense language since you are describing these past events from the reality of your vision and the year from which you are speaking. Have fun with it and just speak it with conviction. There is no harm in speaking what you see.

The last item to share is your Vision Statement. Now ask them for their overall feedback. Don't be surprised if each person begins by asking more in-depth questions about your future, or if they say nothing at all and change the subject. Whatever happens is OK.

Envisioning is a very dynamic process that keeps unfolding. The more you exercise the visionary muscle, the livelier the process becomes. Sharing it is planting the seed, and then we can keep watering and see it emerge and take form.

This exercise of sharing your future with trusted advisors is designed to help you begin to treat your future as fact—as Elise Boulding found was necessary, in her research—by talking about it with people in present-tense language. It also allows you to test the possibility of this desired future as you hear yourself talk about it aloud and receive feedback from people who know you and care about you.

FEEDBACK IS NOT OPEN-ENDED

This is not meant to be an open-ended exercise. This might give too much power away to the people you are sharing with, and you want to stay strong in what you see, even if others don't see it the way you do—yet!

Please read the steps carefully so they can guide you in sharing this burgeoning vision.

It works best when you carefully set the context before getting feedback. Framing your conversation is key to getting helpful input. When I shared, I let my sister know the context (I was asked to do this exercise by the company I was now working for), what I needed her to do (listen and tell me if it resonated with who she knew me to be and if she had questions), and the amount of time it would likely take.

THINGS TO KEEP IN MIND WHEN OBTAINING FEEDBACK

The purpose of sharing is to step out of the private space you've been working in so you can share your vision, and the steps that you see must happen to achieve your vision, with a few trusted people.

- It is important to hear your own voice speaking your vision out loud—it is a critical step to owning your vision and beginning the process of treating it as fact.

- The questions the people you share with may ask will bring more of your vision to the surface of your thinking. This is a good thing.

- Feedback is a gift. Not every gift must be accepted. Most important is to have the conversation. You get to decide what to do with the feedback.

INSTRUCTIONS: FEEDBACK PROCESS

Step 1: **Select two people** as *feedback partners* and ask for a face-to-face meeting. If distance is an obstacle, voice-to-voice would work but video chat would be better. Do not use email or write; it's too one-dimensional for you to get the helpful feedback essential to this step.

Step 2: **Frame your conversation**. Using the outline and questions that follow, begin by expressing your appreciation for their willingness to meet with you and hear about what you are learning about yourself and your future. Explain why you chose them. Explain to them that you are working through a planning process to gain a new approach to your future and you want to share a few of your outcomes with them for their feedback. You might add that you are using a vision technique and you want to share with them one vision of your future that has come out of that, along with a few steps leading up to it.

Share that this is the vision work and before you move ahead to creating your plan (the next step in the process), this step of getting feedback on the work to date is important.

Step 3: **Share the agenda**. Share that this will take about an hour. You will be sharing some of the learning from your foundational work of clarifying who you are that prepared you for the vision work. Then you will share the three parts of your vision work (the vision itself, Visionary Milestones, Vision Statement).

Ask your feedback partners to listen specifically with these questions in mind:

How do you see my vision relating to who you know me to be?

Does it sound like me?

- If it does, why?
- If it doesn't, why not?

What questions do you have?

What feedback or observations do you have?

Step 4: **Share** excerpts from the foundational work you did early in this book and the insight that came from your Four Approaches exercise and your understanding gained from discovering your mission/purpose, core values, significant accomplishments, and strengths and challenges. Share any identified themes that became a context for your vision work. Share your Five Greatest Questions. Share your vision, Visionary Milestones, and Vision Statement.

Step 5: **Capture feedback.** It is important to capture their feedback, their questions, and your answers for your future reference.

FEEDBACK OUTLINE & QUESTIONS

FRAMING

Use these talking points:

- *Thank You:* Thank you so much for taking the time to meet with me!

  I chose you because . . .

  I am working through a planning process to gain a new approach to my future that is more proactive, instead of just waiting for life to happen to me.

- *Outcomes:* I want to share a few outcomes of the process and I'd love to get your feedback. This step of sharing my vision and the work to date before I move ahead to the next step of creating my plan is important.

- *Agenda:* This will take about an hour.

I am asking if you could listen specifically with these questions in mind:

1. How do you see my vision relating to who you know me to be?

2. Does it sound like me? If it does, why? If it doesn't, why not?

3. What questions do you have?

4. What feedback or observations do you have?

SHARING

Share these results from your Strategic Futuring work:

- Insight from the Four Approaches exercise.

- Your mission/purpose, core values, significant accomplishments, and strengths and challenges.

- Themes that emerged as context for your vision.

- Your Five Greatest Questions.

- Visionary Milestones and Vision Statement.

FEEDBACK RECORD ONE

Name of Person Giving Feedback:_____ Date: _____

1. How do you see my vision relating to who you know me to be?

2. Does it sound like me?

   • If it does, why?

   • If it doesn't, why not?

3. What questions do you have?

4. What feedback or observations do you have?

FEEDBACK RECORD TWO

Name of Person Giving Feedback:_____ Date: _____

1. How do you see my vision relating to who you know me to be?

2. Does it sound like me?

   • If it does, why?

   • If it doesn't, why not?

3. What questions do you have?

4. What feedback or observations do you have?

KATHY'S STORY
SPEAKING IS BELIEVING

Ray facilitated Strategic Futuring for Kathy the first time upon referral from Wayne Herron, whose story you read earlier. Hearing some of the similarities in our stories—given that we both came from homes with many rules and somehow had managed to break free of them—Ray encouraged Kathy and me to meet. We were kindred spirits immediately and are close friends to this day.

Kathy comes from a long line of influential women. Along with the influence, there were strings attached and a lot of rules. She has a list of accomplishments a mile long, including being named philanthropist of the year for the City of Los Angeles in 2009. As Kathy clarified her understanding of the power of her own story, she saw how rooted it was in her past and decisions she made when she was young, to go against what was "acceptable" and what she was told to do. She was told she needed to follow the rules. Her father told her, "Kathy, you know you are to obey me. If the drinking water is polluted and I tell you to drink toilet water, you will drink the toilet water." That was the extent to which she was expected to obey—and yet she decided at one point that these rules were not serving her or allowing her to be the compassionate and giving person she knew herself to be. She saw in those around her the logical end of following those rules and she could not stomach it. She chose the road less traveled. In that environment, she was expected to only go to certain schools and to marry within that same social circle. To deviate was not only to go against authority figures, but to risk being literally disowned or cut off from her inheritance. Her inheritance was used as a source of control over her behavior and her life. She described the feeling of constantly "having a hand on my head."

She didn't care what it cost her. She felt her soul was at risk if she didn't do something radical. She recalled a time when she got on a plane to leave for the East Coast without the approval of her parents; she said, "I don't care if the plane crashes—I'll be free!"

As Kathy articulated her vision, it started to become much clearer that she wanted to continue the legacy of her family's stewardship of financial resources and also her own legacy of protecting her own authenticity no matter what external rules seemed to dictate. It was this that she felt was important to pass forward. She saw herself writing a book that shared her story and her family's story so it could be passed forward well beyond her. She saw herself as a painter and artist—someone who expressed herself freely through creativity.

As she began to share especially these two aspects of what she saw with others, they became enrolled in what she saw. She shared them at first timidly and then with more conviction. As I started writing this book, a colleague came alongside her and she now has written her own book that will soon be published called *Claiming Your Voice: Seven Steps to Freedom*.

As she was mentioning her commitment to painting every week, a new store owner requested some of her paintings for display and sale in the store for others to enjoy. She has now sold a dozen paintings! Kathy has always been a courageous rule breaker and creator of her own destiny—going against powerful forces to lay claim to her own sense of herself and what is right. I am inspired by how Kathy continues to choose what is important, envisioning a way forward that is different than what has been modeled and in essence speaks it into reality.

CAPTURE YOUR LEARNING

What was your most significant learning (or observation) from this chapter?

Does your story for the future resonate with what people know of you?

What questions do people have for you about your future?

CONCLUDING THOUGHTS

The beginning of making a vision real is speaking it aloud. The vision then has the opportunity to move beyond a private vision or a dream. When you say it out loud to another person, you will begin to own it. You begin to treat it as fact, as Elise Boulding would say. The more you verbalize it, the more you give it power and allow it the possibility to become a reality. You may already be doing this. Take note of this behavior and your conviction about your vision, even if others don't quite see it the way you do.

After hearing Elise Boulding speak, Ray realized he was, in fact, speaking his vision as fact. When people would ask him what he was going to be doing, he would respond by saying, "**I am going to be** the Dean of Students at a small liberal arts school." He didn't say, "I hope to . . ." or "I'm thinking of . . ." He said, "I am going to be . . ." Others responded very positively to Ray when he spoke that way. They treated it as fact as well and said, "If that is what you're going to do, you need to meet my colleague So-and-so." Or, "You should think about going through this preparation program."

This begins the process of translating our vision into something real. The next piece is beginning to integrate your future direction into your everyday so that even your small daily actions are serving where you see yourself going in the future.

$$\left(\,6\,\right)$$

CREATE YOUR PLAN AND START MOVING

(BE PREPARED FOR UNREASONABLE REQUESTS FROM THE KING)

After I told him of my vision, Ray didn't exactly jump on board with my seemingly crazy idea of running his company in my future, but as any good coach and mentor would do, he turned it into a learning opportunity. He said, if this was a path I wanted to go down, I needed to put together a plan. He said he would help me with ideas to create my plan and would support my plan, as I had specific things for him to do. This is what I did.

For some people, taking action to create a plan is the most exciting part of the whole process. For others this represents a huge hurdle. To them, it is the beginning of making choices and changes that allow the vision to be possible. Either way, this is a place many people get stuck, since it requires taking the vision seriously enough to at least explore how they might achieve such a vision. This is the time to find the pathway to achieve your vision.

LESS IS MORE

I went into this part of the process feeling as if I was learning a foreign language. I overpromised, trying to fit fifteen years' worth of objectives into ninety days. I fumbled around until I found something that worked for me. You do not need to do this perfectly—just describe it in a way that works for you.

I have found that doing less is more—by putting one objective in each Goal Area, it was more manageable for me. Think about focusing on the *one thing* in each of your Goal Areas that will make the most difference in moving toward your vision. This approach is described brilliantly in the book *The ONE Thing: The Surprisingly Simple Truth Behind Extraordinary Results* by Gary Keller and Jay Papasan.[1]

I now encourage my clients to do the same. In my own vision, I also found a lot of value in reviewing my Action Plan with my Strategic Partner, as I will encourage you to do in the next chapter, even though my first attempt at Strategic Partnering did not go as planned (seems to be a theme in life). The process of preparing for the meeting gave me clarity and the confidence to move forward.

CREATE YOUR ROADMAP AND START MOVING

Your Action Plan becomes your roadmap for making your vision a reality.

The Strategic Futuring process is based on a long-range vision. Identifying goals and objectives creates the structure and focus that you will need to take action toward your vision.

The most important step is to start moving! Many people choose to stay parked in the garage until they have it all figured out. Fortunately or unfortunately, as you start moving, you will get more information that helps you adjust. As I've learned the hard way, **it's really hard to steer a parked car.**

You now have a general idea where you are now and where you want to go on the map. Plug the destination coordinates into your GPS. Along the way, you might find a new route you weren't aware of when you started. You may even discover a new destination that is even better than the original. Ray explained that in his own story, his vision was more a doorway to the next phase of life rather than an end in itself. He saw himself becoming Dean of Students and it took him fourteen years to achieve this. Then, he was only in the position for eight months. It was not the destination, but an important door he needed to travel through. Just be aware that it may not be a straight line. There are often many twists and turns.

Even after planting the seed, Paul still watered it and did certain things to create his roadmap—and then he had to course-correct.

For example, his first attempts to get his message out there by taking a more traditional approach to publishing did not work. He stayed strong in his conviction that he was meant to write about this subject and eventually used a very different approach to get his first book on the market. Ironically, he was then approached by a traditional publisher to write his second book!

Your Action Plan is a personal working document. It can keep you focused, remind you of all that you are working toward, help you celebrate successes, and serve as a decision-making tool. Ray carries his Action Plan with him daily. The following suggestions for what to include are the tools and strategies that have worked for countless people, but each person is different—shape your document to fit your needs. It needs to work for you! If you take the time to write it and use it, you may be amazed at the results. It will help you identify your pathway and the necessary support you will need to move toward your vision.

YOUR ACTION PLAN HAS SEVEN COMPONENTS

Put these all together to keep all the important pieces in one place and integrated. Even though you have worked on some of these in other chapters, just bring them forward here so you have a comprehensive context for your plan. Each is defined here.

1. Purpose/Mission Statement

Bring this forward from the Purpose and Mission exercise.

2. Core Values

You worked on core values in the Values exercise. Bring these forward to your Action Plan below and look again at how you have defined these in your everyday actions. How do you know you are living these? This is important to review.

3. Vision Statement

You articulated this in your vision exercise. Bring this forward to your Action Plan, since it will continue to be powerful part of your criteria for decision-making.

> ## Goals:
>
> Goals are directional in nature. (Think of goals like stars;
> they guide your travel or progress.)
> Goals are multi-year.
> Some goals may guide you for an unlimited period of time.

4. Goals

Goals are the large areas of focus that may take two or more years to complete. Some goals will remain on your list indefinitely. One of my goals was to learn the business of consulting, since I saw myself running the business in my future. That was a big area of focus for me and I did something each month toward that larger goal. I still do.

5. Issues, Challenges, and Questions

Some of these will come from the feedback you gathered in the Sharing and Feedback exercise. Some you may not have foreseen and encountered as you have worked toward your goals. These may require expanding your goals in order to overcome them.

New questions may arise as you move forward, and these can be addressed with the help of your Strategic Partner, as you'll learn in the next chapter.

6. Ninety-Day Objectives

Determining the steps necessary to implement a plan may in some ways be the most challenging part of the whole process. These steps create the pathway and the responsibilities for achieving your vision.

Ninety-day objectives are used for two reasons. First, focusing on what can be realistically accomplished over a short period of time brings energy to the process and a sense of accomplishment as you continue to move toward your goals and vision. Second, the world around you changes so rapidly that if you plan too far in the future, you run the risk that your plans become less and less relevant. It's difficult to stay focused and interested in something that seems irrelevant to your life. Think of each of the hunter's quests as a ninety-day objective.

> Objectives:
>
> Objectives are more specific and concrete than goals.
> Objectives concentrate on achieving something within a specific time frame.
> Objectives are intended to be achieved in one year or less.

One objective I had in learning the business of consulting in the early days was very concrete—to join Ray on a consulting project. This helped me learn what he actually did with clients, how he brought in business, and the nature of the business as a whole. Objectives must be concrete so you know that you have achieved them. Goals tend to be a little more open-ended, as mine was with learning an entire industry.

7. Support

As you begin to translate your vision into a plan, it is best to first decide what you need to focus on accomplishing over the next couple of years. Identifying three to five areas of targeted activity allows you to maintain sufficient focus as you begin to implement your vision-driven plan. Goals become strategic when you are intentional about setting ninety-day SMART objectives.

> You need freedom from perceived responsibilities when it comes to creating a vision. But when it comes to making your vision real, you need focus along with the structure and pressure of deadlines.

INSTRUCTIONS: DEVELOP YOUR ACTION PLAN

The following Action Plan outline will assist you in creating the roadmap for your vision.

Step 1: Bring forward your mission and purpose statements, your core values, and your Vision Statement from earlier chapters. Do any needed review of these so they are relevant and powerful as the foundation of your plan!

Step 2: Finalize your goals. The Life Areas (such as health, career, or family) that you identified as key areas of focus in an earlier chapter now will become actual goals. You will also probably add or modify from this initial list.

Step 3: Create your Goal Statements. A Goal Statement is the wording format for your goal. A Goal Statement includes a clear verb, subject, and outcome statement. The outcome statement should express what achieving your goal will accomplish that serves your vision.

Formula for Goal Statement:

Developing (verb) a clear vision-based plan (subject) that will serve as a functional guide for the translation of my vision into reality (outcome statement).

SAMPLE GOAL STATEMENT

I also knew that to run a company I had to learn how to be a good public speaker, so my goal was and still is: *Develop my voice (speaking and writing regularly) and public presence so that I am better positioned to be a recognized thought leader and visible representative of Genysys.*

Step 4: Assess issues, challenges, and questions.

For each Goal Statement that you write, take the time to do a simple assessment of the issues, challenges, and questions as you develop your objectives—and ultimately your Action Plan—around each goal.

For me, my initial assessment just included a few challenges:

- Finding regular time to write—that is good psychological space

- Sticking with a process to get content out and then edit—or send it to others

- Keeping motivated when there may not be the desired response

Step 5: Identify your ninety-day objectives. Once you have all of your Goal Statements identified, write at least one or two SMART objectives that will specifically help you achieve each Goal Statement in your Action Plan in the next ninety days.

S – Specific (it is concrete)

M – Measurable (you know when you've completed it)

A – Achievable (it is realistic)

R – Results-oriented (it will serve your vision)

T – Time bound (there is a deadline)

These SMART objectives will provide the concrete actions that you must work to achieve for each goal.

For example, one of my SMART objectives toward the goal I shared around developing my voice and public presence was to "Complete Toastmasters certification (which includes ten speeches) by December 31, 20XX." There were several tasks related to achieving that objective, but I did it and celebrated with my partners who helped me get there!

Each objective you meet moves you a step closer to your vision, and the energy that comes from accomplishing an objective helps propel you forward to achieve the next objective. It's important to make a realistic assessment as you determine your objectives. This step is easily overlooked, yet vital.

Either once a month or once each ninety-day period, identify the *one thing* in each of your Goal Areas that will make the most difference in moving toward your vision.

Step 6: Either once a month or once each ninety-day period, identify the one thing in each of your Goal Areas that will make the most difference in moving toward your vision. This helps you prioritize the many objectives you may have listed to see the one that will make the biggest impact.

Step 7: Identify the support you need. Don't forget this step, even though it is last! No one can do this alone. Think about the support you may need. It may be in the form of setting aside the money for a particular objective. It may be that the support you need is simply to tell someone what your objective is and give them permission to check in with you.

When I was working on my objective of completing my Toastmasters certification, for each speech, I asked Ray to be my first listener so I could deliver it and get feedback. I also committed to put my next speech on the calendar with Toastmasters so I always had the time pressure of having to prepare. The Toastmasters group kept me accountable to my word and desire on their end.

MY STRATEGIC FUTURING
ACTION PLAN EXERCISE

My purpose/mission statement:

My operationalized core values:

1.

2.

3.

4.

5.

My Vision Statement:

Goal Statement 1:

Issues, challenges, and questions:

SMART objective for this goal (the *one thing* that will make the biggest difference):

The support you will need to overcome challenges:

Goal Statement 2:

Issues, challenges, and questions:

SMART objective for this goal (the *one thing* that will make the biggest difference):

The support you will need to overcome challenges:

Goal Statement 3:

Issues, challenges, and questions:

SMART objective for this goal (the *one thing* that will make the biggest difference):

The support you will need to overcome challenges:

Goal Statement 4:

Issues, challenges, and questions:

SMART objective for this goal (the *one thing* that will make the biggest difference):

The support you will need to overcome challenges:

KATHLEEN'S STORY
JUST MOVE

Ray's wife, Mary-Ellen, told me for years this story of a manicurist/phlebotomist-turned-chef and I thought this woman must be a fictional character. When I met Kathleen and interviewed her for this book, I was amazed that this woman really did, in fact, exist and that her story was just as powerful as Mary-Ellen described. Kathleen just took things one step at a time, seemingly building her bridge while she walked on it.

Kathleen was a manicurist and also a phlebotomist at the local hospital to pay the bills and raise her children as a single mother. She was in her early forties and her children were almost grown when a long-time client of hers (Mary-Ellen) coached her through the Strategic Futuring process. She realized she had always wanted to be a professional chef, but didn't know if she could do it or if she could support herself financially as a chef. She had always cooked for her family and thoroughly enjoyed experimenting with different combinations that tantalized the taste buds. She saw herself owning a restaurant, bringing joy to people with her innovative food creations.

Mary-Ellen remembers Kathleen was stuck at one point and didn't know how she could pay for school or get the knives she needed for class. She told her father being a chef was what she really wanted to do. He was surprised, but wanted to support her vision. Her planned next step was to go to culinary school.

When her father heard this, he offered to gift her the knives she needed for class.

Kathleen went to culinary school and ended up being the personal chef for President Gerald Ford and his wife for several years. Then in 2015, Kathleen opened her own restaurant in Palm Springs, California, with her brother, called Serious Food and Drink. When I asked her how she dared to take the leap to do what she saw, she said, "Do you mean, how was I so stupid?"

I laughed and told her I've felt the exact same way. Some days I feel like the smartest person and others I feel I must be stupid for going after my vision, with so much at risk. That feeling can change by the day.

Kathleen's story illustrated to me just how powerful Strategic Futuring can be in affirming one's commitment to be themselves and find a way to make a living doing what they love, despite how silly it may feel at times. The most important thing has been to just keep moving—keep planning and revising the plan. Keep getting input from others about, "If I want to do this, how do I get there?" That is what helped Kathleen pursue her dream, one step at a time.

CAPTURE YOUR LEARNING

Take a few moments here to respond to the following questions:

What has been your most significant learning from this chapter?

Was there anything surprising?

What did you learn about yourself (or have affirmed in a new way)
by going through this exercise?

CONCLUDING THOUGHTS

It's hard to steer a parked car. When you have a general roadmap and a way to locate where you are, you just need to keep moving, even though you may not even know if the next step will appear. It is like Robert Quinn talks about in his book *Building the Bridge as You Walk on It: A Guide for Leading Change.*[2] As scary as that is, staying in the garage will not help you figure out where to go. You must be in search of your next quest. I am reminded that if the hunter hadn't gotten out of bed that morning and been about his business, he would not have been in the forest at the right time to come upon the Golden Feather. As you keep moving and keep your plan in constant conversation with what is really happening, you gain more clarity about your vision and the pathway to what you really want.

7

PARTNER FOR SUCCESS: ENROLL YOUR HORSE

Past is experience, present is experiment, and future is expectation. Use your experience in your experiments to achieve your expectations.

—Nishan Panwar

My sister had a vision and just like always, I was her loyal horse holding the vision with her. I was thirteen years old, standing on the fireplace "stage," waiting for my brother's grand entrance in his full-length ruffled, lacy turquoise-blue dress. My sister had the performance all planned out in her head, and, as usual, I was "all in" to make it happen. She had enrolled me in the vision of what it could be. My poor brother didn't really have a choice. We put on a show that was a masterpiece! My sister recalled recently that she always appreciated how I came alongside her when she had these visions and I was excited to help her make them real when all my other siblings just tolerated her ideas.

If you're wondering who to share your vision with, you are not alone. A horse often shows up unexpectedly, and can sometimes ask you what seem to be strange or annoying questions that get your attention. Ray showed up that way for me. In one of my graduate classes, he asked me if other people saw me as a leader at work. I had never thought about that. And it was an important realization.

Quite often, for over ninety percent of my clients, someone at Genysys becomes their horse. But why do you need a horse? If you remember from the Golden Feather story, the hunter was riding the horse and then when he came upon the feather, the horse spoke up. Before that moment, he saw his horse quite differently—and then when the horse spoke, he began to see him as a guide, or even a mentor. Your horse might already be a part of your journey and may also speak up unexpectedly. If that happens, you will likely have a different conversation with this person than you have had previously.

What makes a great horse?

- Asks questions or makes provocative statements that can be confrontational in nature.

- Gives wisdom and insight about the road ahead.

- Is willing to go with you on the journey, whether you heed their advice or not.

As I was attempting to put my Action Plan together, it seemed overwhelming. In fact, I put it in a drawer to avoid it. It felt too big, out of reach, and I wasn't used to having dreams, let alone figuring out how to make them a reality. When I was forced to have my next meeting with Ray, I begrudgingly pulled it out of the drawer and forced an attempt at preparing a plan. As soon as we sat down, I admitted I didn't get it and needed his help to get clarity. Bringing ideas from distant thoughts to goals was a major step for me. My vision was to lead a company in fifteen years. Knowing I would need to be the face of the company, a goal became to learn how to be a great public speaker. To that end, I decided I should get my Toastmasters certification (ten speeches) from my Ice Breaker speech (#1) to the Inspire Your Audience speech (#10). The necessary support I identified was to have someone I trusted (a horse) listen to the first draft of my speeches and give me feedback. I asked Ray to partner with me on this and he was more than willing. For every speech I drafted and presented to Ray, he explained what he liked and what I should change. If I was stuck on how to start, he would give advice such as, "If it were me, this is what I would say . . ." This was incredibly helpful and after each speech, I summarized for Ray how it went, and we would celebrate the completion. When I got my Toastmasters certification, it felt like a huge accomplishment!

When I was in the Feedback Stage, I was looking for my Strategic Partners. A couple of attempts didn't work so well, but I learned from those experiences what I really needed from my partners (horses). Don't be discouraged if the first horse you approach isn't the one you end up with. For me, it has been great to partner with people who have already gone through the Strategic Futuring process, since they know the process and want to gain support for their own plans as well.

Ray was a great horse for me—he asked me a lot of thought-provoking questions and gave me a lot of feedback about my vision, especially since leading his company was a part of it (awkward!). Even though he didn't buy the idea one hundred percent at the beginning, he supported my vision and went along with it. To achieve your goals, you need the help and support of others! In the Strategic Futuring process, you need the intentional support from those few people identified as *Strategic Partners*. "Strategic" just means these are intentional relationships and not open-ended. They are serving a specific purpose. The word partner is used because successful relationships are always a two-way street. A Strategic Partner is more than a simple accountability partner. In a partnership, both people are gaining something from the relationship.

In a Strategic Partnership, both people have the opportunity to state what they need and want from the relationship. You might be the one to initiate the partnership for the completion of your goals and objectives, but it is not all about you. Through the entire Strategic Futuring journey you have undertaken, there has been an underlying theme of intentionality. That theme continues as you look outwards to the people in your life to identify who you want walking with you toward the achievement of your goals. The idea is to develop a specific and purposeful win-win partnership.

The following Strategic Partnering exercise is designed to help you find your horse and create a partnership. In this exercise, you will incorporate your Action Plan into your real life. By surrounding your plan with support and accountability, your plan stops being an internal exercise and starts becoming real, witnessed, and engaged by more people than just you. That's what happened when I started going to Toastmasters and before I knew it, my vision began to become very real. Your circle will widen and the resources and actions you have identified will now begin to play out where others can see and participate in what you are creating. For some, this exercise will be challenging, because it can be scary to share with others what you see when you are in the beginning of believing it yourself. Whatever your approach, this is the beginning of living your plan.

INSTRUCTIONS: FINDING YOUR STRATEGIC PARTNERS

Using the steps below, pick two people to be your partners for the next six months. You may enjoy the process so much, you may decide to continue it—but it is important to have an initial period of commitment in the relationship.

Choosing your partners is a thoughtful process. These individuals will serve as a sort of personal advisory board. You will share your plan with each of them, one-to-one, in a structured way, and solicit their feedback and support. By doing this on a routine basis, you will also create an accountability system to keep you honest and on track. The hunter would go on a journey, then check in with his horse at the end of every journey before going on to the next. The horse would say, "No, this still isn't the fear and trouble I'm talking about, but I'll help you get out of what you've gotten us into." Warning—you may not like what your horse says. No lasting success can be built and sustained by just one person. Your support and the accountability you create through these unique relationships are your keys to success.

Remember, your vision is sacred and it is still emerging. Choose carefully! The people you pick through this exercise will support your Action Plan and, specifically, your ninety-day SMART objectives. Consider whom you most trust and respect, and whom you consider to be wise, understanding, and supportive.

Step 1: **Consider your contacts.**

This is a time for exercising all your wisdom and integrity in relationships. Make a list of **all** the people you might consider sharing your plan with at this stage. Keep in mind, you are going to meet formally with each of the them, once a month, for a period of time you will choose together—at least six months, and up to one year. At that point, it will be essential that you review your support and accountability team for what is working and what isn't. At the end of your agreed-upon time, you may wish to continue with the same people, or be ready for new engagements.

Step 2: Review your resources and your list, and choose your Strategic Partners.

Go back through your Action Plan. Focus on your ninety-day SMART objectives (your quests), and review the support you are ready to receive. What areas do you need to grow? What resources do you need? What are your obstacles? Who on your list will have the interest, ability, and willingness to reliably support you? What specifically will you ask from them?

It's important to consider how you and the partners you choose are similar and different, in your approaches to work, life, and challenges. If you choose people who have strengths where you have challenges, they may be of valuable assistance in helping you overcome those. Similarities can also be a benefit, if you share the same core values.

Be prepared to share your thinking with each person you select. This helps them understand better how to support you and how to bring accountability into your conversation. It will help them see you are taking yourself and your dreams seriously, and show your level of investment in your own process. You will also be sharing your trust and respect, which will strengthen the relationship.

Step 3: Extend your invitations.

When you have selected your two people, call or email them to ask them to join you on the adventure. Here's some sample language:

For the last ____ weeks I've been learning to use a Strategic Futuring tool that has helped me see a vision for my future and take practical steps that can make my vision real. I'm at the stage in the process when I need to bring in some trusted friends for support and accountability. I really thought hard about who I wanted on this journey with me, and I'm wondering if you would be willing to be one of my support partners? It will involve meeting with me once a month for the next six months. And I can explain in detail exactly what I'll ask of you when we meet or talk next. Would you let me know if you are interested in going on this journey with me?

When you arrange to meet, be very clear that in the first meeting you will need time to cover the following agenda:

- Share with them the steps of Strategic Futuring and what the process has meant for you—as much or little detail as you wish. Remember the steps are

    Step 1: Choose to own your story

    Step 2: Dare to ask the right questions

    Step 3: See and speak your vision

    Step 4: Create your Action Plan

    Step 5: Partner for success

- **Review** with them your vision, Action Plan, goals, and specifically your ninety-day SMART objectives.

- Share again the **reasons you selected them** as your support and accountability partner.

- Share the types of **support you will ask** of them (insight, wisdom, advice, reflection, opinions, direction, trouble-shooting, resources identification, connections, tools or mechanisms, clarification, honesty, brainstorming—think carefully about what you need from each unique person. You don't have to anticipate it all, but a little will be helpful).

- Share with them the three questions you will discuss at every meeting (see the meeting form):

  · What has happened since we last met?

  · What do I need to focus on this month to move toward my goals?

  · Looking at my goals and challenges, what support is needed to keep moving forward, and how is that obtained?

- Identify together all the things you'll need to **be aware of** as you meet (similarities, strengths, differences, challenges, etc.).

- Ask **what they need from you** to make this a satisfying and rewarding exchange for them.

- Emphasize that a large part of their role is to **celebrate** your accomplishments with you!

- Ask them to **sign** your form—a formality required by your program facilitator.

Make sure you allow enough time for such a full agenda, and keep your conversation focused.

Step 4: First meeting.

Your first meeting will cover the agenda above. Make sure you bring their contract, with your portion already filled in, and a pen.

Decide ahead of time where in your agenda you want to bring forward your contract. It may seem silly to be so formal, especially if they are a close friend or family member, but it makes a *huge* difference in the quality of the commitment, the focus of the conversation, and the seriousness of the outcomes. Your vision of your future is now fully in play. Don't shortchange yourself and all your hard work to date—get the signature. And don't forget to celebrate this commitment—these are big first steps into your emerging reality.

Before you finish your meeting, schedule your next progress review. Don't leave a meeting without setting up the next one.

Step 5: Maintenance between meetings.

Before each Strategic Partnering meeting, glance through your Action Plan and thoughtfully organize your reflections on your progress and specific questions for your next round of review. This demonstrates your respect for your own work and the process.

When you meet again, make sure to present what you've prepared. *Cover your three points each time.* Report your progress and seek their feedback.

Be sure to express your gratitude to your Strategic Partner and their investment of time and energy in you and your future.

Lastly, remember to set new SMART objectives every ninety days or sooner when needed.

STRATEGIC PARTNERING EXERCISE

This exercise is your quick reference for the steps you'll take to choose and connect with your Strategic Partners. List the two people you would like to support you as you implement your Action Plan:

1.

2.

Articulate the kind of support you would like from them and why you would like them to be in a partnership with you on this journey. Be as specific as possible. The detail you identify in these two questions will be important as you initiate these partnerships!

Strategic Partner 1:

Support needed:

Why this person specifically:

Similarities and differences compared to you:

Strategic Partner 2:

Support needed:

Why this person specifically:

Similarities and differences compared to you:

PARTNERING AGREEMENT 1

Strategic Partnering Agreement

Between _____ and _____
                (You)   (Strategic Partner)

We agree to meet _____ per month for _____ months
                      (at least once)   (6 or 12)

at_____ at _____ on _____
            (location)   (time)   (day of week)

When we meet, we will discuss action and progress toward two- to three-year goals and current SMART objectives. We will also celebrate Action Plan progress and accomplishments.

Specifically, we will cover these three questions:

1. What has taken place since we last met?

2. What do I (initiating partner) need to focus on this month, in order to move toward my goals?

3. Looking at my goals and challenges, what support is needed to keep moving forward?

These one to two things are most important for us to know about each other's similarities and differences as we partner:

- _____

- _____

_____   _____
      Your signature   Strategic Partner's signature

Date: _____   Date: _____

PARTNERING AGREEMENT 2

Strategic Partnering Agreement

Between _____ and _____
              (You)   (Strategic Partner)

We agree to meet _____ per month for _____ months
                    (at least once)   (6 or 12)

at_____ at _____ on _____
            (location)   (time)   (day of week)

When we meet, we will discuss action and progress toward two- to three-year goals and current SMART objectives. We will also celebrate Action Plan progress and accomplishments.

Specifically, we will cover these three questions:

1. What has taken place since we last met?

2. What do I (initiating partner) need to focus on this month, in order to move toward my goals?

3. Looking at my goals and challenges, what support is needed to keep moving forward?

These one to two things are most important for us to know about each other's similarities and differences as we partner:

- _____

- _____

_____   _____
        Your signature   Strategic Partner's signature

Date: _____   Date: _____

ILENE'S STORY
THE POWER OF OUR PARTNERS

I knew Ilene Bezjian only by her stellar reputation around campus, when we worked at the same university. She was also my dean as I was getting my master's degree in the School of Business. When I actually got acquainted with Ilene, she was transitioning out of the dean position and was looking for her next move. Ilene had been in the same job for fifteen years, during which she reached her personal goals and felt very good about the way she had also helped the organization progress. When a major organizational change occurred, she realized it was time for her also to make a change. She couldn't see herself doing anything but the job she'd had for the past decade and a half. Feeling that she was no longer a "spring chicken," she wondered where her skills would be useful. At that point, her husband ran into Ray Rood on campus and suggested she go through the Strategic Futuring process.

A big "aha" moment came for Ilene as she looked at the Four Approaches to the Future. She realized that as the organization's administration had changed their direction to a more reactive approach, she was expected to react. In turn, her approach to her life, including her work, had become more reactive. Her natural instinct was to use a proactive or inventive approach, which caused tension and distrust within the organization. It was clear she needed a change of environment.

She went through her vision work not just by herself, but with her husband, Vic. They did the work separately and then did a "reveal" each week to share what they saw when they met with Ray. I joined the conversation when they were sharing their visions of the future, and it was amazing to hear what they were learning about each other, even after being married for thirty-five years. They were heading in the same direction for their futures, and they both had big ideas about what they wanted to be doing. Ilene wanted to use her experience to impact international business education, and Vic wanted to leverage his tenure in the military to start a nonprofit that would help other veterans see a way from military into civilian life.

Ilene had spoken previously about being unable to see how she could use her skills in a meaningful way outside of an institution, however, after going through Strategic Futuring, she was able to see a way to have a major impact as a consultant without the formal structures she had been accustomed to for the past two decades.

As Ilene put together her plan and then assembled her partners—including her husband—she started to see how her vision could begin to unfold by taking steps each day. She continued to refine her path forward and celebrate successes, both small and large, in the midst of the challenges of Vic's deployments.

"Are you making the amount of money you set out to make?" That was the question one of Ilene's Strategic Partners asked her. To me, this showed how strong Ilene's Strategic Partnership was because Ilene's partner wanted to ensure that what Ilene had envisioned was being translated into concrete terms and that

Ilene had the support she needed to continue moving toward her vision. Her partner called her every Monday to check in with her on her plan. Not only did she check in with her on her progress, but she asked her those hard questions. This stood out to me as a very healthy partnership.

CAPTURE YOUR LEARNING

Take ten minutes to reflect on what you learned from this chapter.

What has been your most significant learning from this chapter (something that was surprising, new, or that you already knew but was affirmed in a new way)?

What did you learn as you initiated and made Strategic Partnership agreements?

CONCLUDING THOUGHTS

When we find people that we are intentional in connecting with on a regular basis, it makes all the difference in our ability to be successful. Earlier in this process, you were asked to answer the question, "Will this happen?" This now becomes the central question as you conclude your Strategic Futuring training.

Remember, Elise Boulding would say it will happen to the extent that you treat your vision as fact, including taking it seriously enough to gain the support you need from your horses. This helps you create the conditions for attaining your vision!

Boulding could see a world of peace and was nominated for the Nobel Peace Prize in 1990 because of her dedication to helping others see peace as well and creating a pathway where world peace could become a reality. Boulding was not alone in her quest. She had amazing partners, including her husband, who worked closely with her to bring her own vision of making an impact for peace to fruition.

As you think of other famous partners such as Ben and Jerry (Ben Cohen and Jerry Greenfield) or Hewlett and Packard (Bill Hewlett and Dave Packard), they may seem inseparable from the other. It is important to remember that as you move forward with your vision, you are better with your wise horse at your side. As the famous African proverb goes, "If you want to go fast, go alone. If you want to go far, go together."

8

BE THE HORSE: HELP OTHERS SEE THEIR GOLDEN FEATHER

By having the courage to change themselves, they model the behavior they are asking of others.

—Robert Quinn, *Deep Change: Discovering the Leader Within*[1]

In 2010, the phone rang. It was Ray. He said, "Priscilla, I think your vision is unfolding a little sooner than you might have anticipated."

My ears perked up and I began to realize that the vision I had created for fifteen years in the future was now becoming a reality. I had really begun to take my vision seriously at this point. Like you may, while you are on this journey, I had been enjoying the process and the rewards for clarity, the increased energy, the possibilities, and the opportunities that had appeared in my life—

but I hadn't fully believed in the process until that moment on the phone. Over the years, I have seen so many people—friends, family, coworkers—going through this process and having results like mine: transformation in their lives. They all needed courage to take the journey.

It takes courage to take the time to dream, to even contemplate having a vision, when all you can think about is the next day, the next hour, or maybe just the next vacation. When you do, amazing possibilities can show up in your life as they did in mine. This journey, which began in 2006, was a journey of synchronicity. I don't know how you found this book, but I can guarantee there was synchronicity at play in how it got into your hands.

The questions in this book will help you to begin to help other people unlock their vision so they can begin to see the future too. Some of the questions that you've learned are . . .

What will I be doing that's going to make an impact on my community or the larger world? What does my family look like? How am I relating to people and having a positive impact? Where should I live that I will enjoy? What work will I be doing that I love?

The question that impacted me the very most in my classes with Ray was, "Do you see yourself as a leader? Do other people see you as a leader?" No matter what role you're playing, you have the opportunity to show up as a leader—first as a leader of yourself. I encourage you to help others to see that their most important Golden Feather is the leading of their life. As you're walking along the path, point out and use these powerful questions and tools to help other people wake up and begin to see the vision of their life. You can use these questions and tools in your work.

As a manager, I would often ask my employees where they wanted to be professionally and how I could support them. So often, people spend time where they're focusing on what's not working. I learned that *organizations can become much more effective when individuals are clear about what they want and how the organization can be a vehicle for them to carry out their career aspirations.*

It's really refreshing and eye-opening to actually shift gears into what else is possible. I began to recognize, as I was on this journey, how important this work can be for organizations. If you're a part of an organization, perhaps you can begin to encourage people to use these questions to shape the organization so the organization can be more cohesive and can make a big impact on all of the individuals that are part of it.

Through your Strategic Futuring experience, you have gathered tools for planning and understanding yourself and your unique contribution to the world.

Step 1: *Choose* to own your story

Step 2: Dare to ask the big questions

Step 3: See and speak your vision

Step 4: Create your Action Plan

Step 5: Partner for success

You have learned the power of accountability through Strategic Partnerships to achieve your vision and make your greatest contribution to the world. Now is the time for you to begin to experience the life you have envisioned. You may be very surprised by how well and how quickly it unfolds.

As you set out living the life you have envisioned and planned, it is important to understand how people grow. Ray Rood, founder of The Genysys Group and the developer of the Strategic Futuring process, offers his philosophy on how people grow, develop, and achieve their goals.

> One of the beliefs central to those of us within the Genysys community is that human development is best pursued and realized when there is a balance between the elements of challenge and support in one's life. Too much challenge and not enough support result in feeling overwhelmed and eventually burnt out, when making even a desired change in life. On the other hand, too much support and not enough challenge results in feeling bored and becoming stagnant, even if one was once energized in any given activity. When we work with clients, we acknowledge the challenge/support matrix to help people locate themselves.
>
> —Ray Rood

Challenge always precedes support, sometimes for an extended period of time. However, there is always more support available if you take the time to identify exactly what you need and then begin the process of looking and asking for what you need. This is sometimes a difficult thing to do, especially if you pride yourself on being self-reliant.

DIFFERENT WAYS TO USE STRATEGIC FUTURING

MINI-FUTURING

Mini-futuring is a simplified Strategic Futuring process that you can take anyone through—you could do it all in one sitting, or you could just ask people the questions below as a normal part of conversation. Get comfortable with the questions so they don't sound forced. You could even show them this book and let them know that this process has really helped you clarify your goals. Ask if they want to do a mini version to see if it helps them gain clarity about a particular issue they are wrestling with.

MINI-FUTURING EXERCISE

If you want to use this tool to help other people or refresh a specific area of your life—work, a relationship with a family member, etc.—answer these questions about this topic:

- What is your greatest accomplishment in this area?

- What is your best skill or strength in this area?

- What do you care about and value most in the area?

- What is your biggest challenge in this area?

- As you look ten years from now, what is your greatest question about this area?

- Imagine you are in the year ____ (ten years from now when you are ____ years old); what does this area look like?

- Now coming back to today, what is one thing you need to focus on to move toward what you imagined? What is the one thing you could do this month that would make the most difference?

- Who can help you accomplish this one thing?
  What kind of support do you need from this person?

WHEN PERSONAL AND COMPANY VISIONS ALIGN

Ray had been working with companies for thirty years and had come to realize that very often personal vision and company vision dovetail—and that's exactly what happened when we were working with a civil engineering company that was going through a leadership transition. The leader of the organization had determined he would not be running the company forever. In fact, he had promised his wife he would have a plan for the company by age fifty-five. When he was age fifty-four, he started looking for someone to help him with creating his plan for the future. A colleague introduced him to Genysys, knowing that Genysys did a lot of planning and transition work for small businesses.

The owner was clear he did not want to just sell it to an outsider. After one of the key executives left the company, the leader was approached by a group of several younger employees. They told him that they wanted to take on the leadership of the company and eventually own the company themselves, rather than being led by a new executive that he would hire. He was very surprised, but after talking with Ray, he saw that he would not likely have another opportunity like this. The operations manager was a young woman named Lucy Gonzalez. She had a lot of energy and she was all about action. She had worked with the young engineers to put together a plan for this "coup," which the owner began to call it. It was in this context that Lucy and I worked together to complete Lucy's Strategic Futuring process. Lucy knew she wanted to be a part of the company, but couldn't quite see the role she wanted to have, other than to help "the guys." Doing the vision work, she saw herself as an equal partner in the engineering business, representing the operational/business side, with her partner representing the engineering side.

She had been working to trust herself and put herself forward as a partner, understanding that this was what she wanted for herself. This had been an internal battle for her as a female in a male-dominated industry and an engineering-centric company, where the business side was not always on equal ground with the engineering. However, as her vision became clearer, she continued to take risky steps to put forward what she saw, gaining the trust of the owner and future ownership, and positioned herself as a key asset in the future of the company.

STRATEGIC FUTURING FOR COMPANIES

Organizations are just complex organisms run by complex humans. Individuals can help organizations change, when they understand the process of change and particularly the role that vision plays in any kind of meaningful change. Most organizations today have either lived beyond or lost their original vision. As a result, they find themselves trying to survive in a reactionary mode while living in the midst of an increasingly challenging and diverse world. Just think if these companies had continued to react. They may not be around today. AOL began as a video on-demand service. Twitter started as a podcast delivery service. Tiffany & Co. sold paper.

The challenge for today's organizational leaders is to create a new vision for their organization to avoid just trying to survive in reactionary mode. They don't have to start over, but if they are to successfully lead their organizations into an ever-changing future, they must be willing to come together to create an initial common vision of the future. Then, they must invite all those who represent the company to join them in expanding the vision over time, until it touches every part of the organization. Such a process enables the organization to not only survive change, but thrive because of change. The organization is then able to move beyond simply reacting to problems and challenges to a place where problems and challenges are viewed in terms of how they serve the organizational vision. In doing so, vision links strategy and culture together in the achievement of organizational effectiveness.

Strategic Futuring for organizations mirrors the individual process and starts with identifying a group of organizational "stakeholders"—those that care about the company and see themselves as having a vested interest in the organization's present and future well-being. These individuals need to be willing to think about the possible future beyond five years. The stakeholders must be willing to share and listen to each other's perspectives in order to find points of common ground and, ultimately, a shared vision. Finally, the stakeholders need to be willing to translate their common vision into a strategic plan where vision interacts with current needs and opportunities in order to choose a direction that is both reality-based and future-focused.

VISIONING FOR COMPANIES

In preparation for vision work, develop three to five subjects or questions for use in developing the vision. What do the leaders/ stakeholders want to know about the future, and/or what strategic issues/questions need to be addressed in choosing a direction? These subjects or questions then serve as the guide for the envisioning process, similar to that for the individual process.

As the stakeholders prepare to build a shared company vision, they will review

- The history (how we came to exist);
- The purpose (why we exist);
- The mission (our focus);
- The guiding core values (our principles of operation); and,
- The needs, trends, and challenges (our opportunities for change).

This review enables the future vision to be built on both the past and present reality.

Then, stakeholders will be ready to envision what the organization will look like and how it will be operating ten years in the future. As individual stakeholders share and integrate their individual visions, a shared vision will begin to emerge, usually full of much more common ground than anyone would have initially believed possible.

Using the answers to the above five questions as the frame for the vision work, the group of stakeholders will use a methodology of incorporating individual reflection, small group discussion, and reporting of themes to develop a vision and Visionary Milestones that are the collective work of the group. They report this work using present-tense language, just the way you would for the individual work. This creates a powerful synergy for a group as they hear the story of the future of the company, reported as if it has already taken place! They create goal candidates that become the framework for their strategic plan and end the vision work by identifying candidate Vision Statements.

OUTCOMES

Other organizational outcomes of a Strategic Futuring planning process include:

- An increased level of positive, collaborative contribution to the future on the part of all who choose to participate;

- An increased sense of ownership among individuals and satisfaction on the part of those who participate, resulting in a greater feeling of individual responsibility for and contribution to the organization's present and future well-being;

- The basis for a vision-directed strategic plan with goals and objectives that can enable the organization to not only anticipate its future but to influence if not create it, as well; and

- Increased organizational effectiveness whereby the mission and purpose is carried out more easily and consistently, resulting in more needs being met and exceeded expectations by both internal and external clients.

Organizational effectiveness is increased when the organizational stakeholders (those organizational members who perceive themselves as having a vested interest in both the organization's present and future well-being) take responsibility for the organization's future.

Organizations have to go through the same essential steps of the Strategic Futuring process:

1. Choose to own their story (including history, mission, core values)

2. Dare to ask their greatest questions

3. Envision their future and speak it out—focusing on common ground

4. Create their Action Plan

5. Develop their internal and external partners

NOW THE ADVENTURE TRULY BEGINS

Choosing your life changes who you are, how you see yourself, and how you're "showing up." People will take note and it may change relationships. It only takes one side of the relationship to change for the relationship dynamic to change.

As you learn how to claim your authenticity and lead your own life and career, you have the opportunity to help others see and make their best contributions. You can help them see the angel within and set it free. In addition, you have the opportunity to be a change agent in organizations or in your community by utilizing the same guiding principles and tools for the organizations as you do for yourself. They are all elements that allow all of us to live intentional and engaged lives, and we can help others do the same and even impact our larger community with these highly adaptive tools that facilitate change. ***Be forewarned—picking up the Golden Feather in your life can be more disruptive than you might anticipate.*** I have found a few notable ways this is the case.

- People will be drawn to you because of your authenticity.

- People may avoid you because you represent authenticity they might rather avoid.

- You may be viewed as an asset because of the insightful question you ask.

- You may be viewed as a threat because you are asking questions people do not know how to answer and have never asked.

- You may feel free and on the cutting edge.

- You may feel alone as you go forth first where others have not dared to go.

As much as this choice is in fact dangerous, I would not do things differently. Remember that if you do not choose the future, the future chooses you. For me, I choose to be the one in charge.

As Ray invited me and my classmates to pick up the Golden Feathers in our lives and choose to lead, I offer you the same challenge. If you dare . . . just know that you will know fear and trouble like you've never known before. However, it is also the path to being truly alive. Know that you are not alone. You are joining a conspiracy—a tribe of rule breakers / rule creators and risk-takers that choose to be themselves, without apology.

EPILOGUE

—By Raymond Rood

All good stories are made up of endings, which in their own way are beginnings to new chapters. Congratulations on taking the time to invest in your future as you continue to write your story and lay claim to your authenticity. This will be the greatest gift you can give yourself. Treat this Strategic Futuring experience as the preface to a powerfully unfolding future that will be transformational in nature, to the extent that you continue to clarify and choose. Strategic Futuring is a way of life.

It will take discipline to integrate such a process into your present lifestyle. This is why your Strategic Partners play such an important role in this journey. Don't expect most people to understand this process, since they may still believe the future chooses them— and they point to their lives as a testimony to that belief. They believe that the future is the author of their story. The philosophy of Strategic Futuring holds that we can at least be the coauthor of our stories. Hopefully one of these days, we can hear something of your story and what you have discovered along the way.

In the meantime, keep the words of the poet Robert Frost in the front of your mind as you continue to choose your future.

Two roads diverged in a wood, and I—
I took the one less traveled by,
and that has made all the difference.[1]

Raymond Rood
Founder, The Genysys Group, Inc.

ABOUT STRATEGIC FUTURING

STRATEGIC FUTURING IS A STEP-BY-STEP PROCESS

Each step of the Strategic Futuring process is intentional and based on proven human development and adult learning theories. It is our belief that any new learning experience will be enhanced if it is based on proven theories and intentional processes.

STRATEGIC FUTURING IS REFLECTIVE

Reflection, especially constructive self-reflection, is an uncommon thought process for most people. Each question is designed to help you dig deeper and address more relevant information than you probably would on your own. This method will make your experience even more meaningful.

STRATEGIC FUTURING REQUIRES PARTNERSHIP

You can envision and write the most amazing and ambitious plans, yet without accountability, the plan quickly becomes meaningless. Even after the process is completed, be sure you have your Strategic Partners in place and also join the Strategic Futurists Facebook group to continue gaining insights and accountability in your journey.

THE STRATEGIC FUTURING PROCESS

Strategic Futuring starts by looking far enough into the future—five years is the typical limit of predictability and responsibility most people experience (and the limit of most strategic planning). To deeply access your sense of possibility, you must access your imagination beyond those constraints, to fifteen years, where there is freedom to explore a more expansive view of life.

Then, the process will help you complete five important perspective-altering steps:

Step 1: *Choose* to own your story

Step 2: Dare to ask the right questions

Step 3: See and speak your vision

Step 4: Create your Action Plan

Step 5: Partner for success

WHO IS STRATEGIC FUTURING FOR?

Strategic Futuring has been helpful to people who are in life stage transitions from college to post-college, from marriage into parenthood, from career into retirement. It is also helpful for people in work-related transitions—after a job loss or while in an unsatisfying job, during a self-motivated career change, and for people in a relationship transition such as divorce, marriage, parenthood, or an empty nest.

Even if there are no transitions on your horizon today, this tool will challenge and inspire you to become fully engaged in life while preparing for the changes that will affect your life.

The Strategic Futuring process begins with the following assumptions:

1. Your life is a story only you can tell.

2. Your story begins at birth and you live your story one day at a time.

3. Along the way, you are presented with challenges, opportunities, threats, and choices in every stage of the life cycle.

4. By looking at the past and assessing the present, you can begin to identify a chosen future.

One of the best-kept secrets is that each person has the ability to influence the future to the extent that you:

- Envision your future
- Treat your vision as fact
- Plan for its realization

STRATEGIC FUTURING OUTCOMES

When a vision is translated to a plan with real goals and short-term actions, the possibility of dreams coming true becomes real. In fact, a powerful vision can become a self-fulfilling prophecy, just as the lack of vision or vision without a sturdy Action Plan can also become a self-fulfilling prophecy. An actionable vision provides criteria for decision-making, both short- and long-term, and helps illuminate how each choice impacts or serves that vision. Finally, a clear vision of the future provides a powerful new perspective on opportunities and challenges as they arise.

Everyone had dreams and visions as children. You may have either outlived your original vision, or feel you have lost it all together. Some people never had that joy or hope. Even in the best cases, it can be hard for your best self to survive by exclusively using the reactionary, responsive, and innovative decision-making modes as you navigate an increasingly challenging world, no matter how successful you might appear on the outside. But you have the option to reengage your dreams and powerfully choose your future. Strategic Futuring is a power tool for building real dreams.

ACKNOWLEDGMENTS

First, thank you, Ray Rood, for your unwavering belief in me for entrusting me with authoring this first Genysys publication. Thank you for putting up with the way I went about it and how messy it has been to figure out how to get this done. It is a significant milestone in our succession journey and I could not have found a better partner in this work. I know this is just one of many ways we will continue to deliver your wisdom to the world. You are truly one-of-a-kind and without apology. Thank you for modeling this for me and countless others through your own commitment to authenticity. Your work has given many people permission to break free of their cages and live more vibrant lives with better opportunities to contribute to this world.

I am grateful to Mary-Ellen Rood, who will say very clearly that she has been a part of every iteration of the business and stayed by Ray and me as we have partnered together to build a "real" company, which is the culmination of both our visions. Mary-Ellen, this would not be happening without your steady support and all of your questions that continue to clarify what this work is really about and why it is so important.

I am grateful to my family for their curiosity along the way and for letting me share some stories from our history and what we have learned as a family to help others gain more power in their lives! Love to Dad (Ted Padwe), Mom (Gail Padwe), my sisters and sister-in-law (Julianne Puckett, Marilee Johnson, Amy Polson, and Jenna Padwe), my brothers and brothers-in-law (Stephen Padwe, Ryan Padwe, Chris Puckett, Dwight Johnson, and John Polson), and all my sweet nieces and nephews.

I want to express my gratitude to the late Elise Boulding. Without her presentation at NASPA in 1982, Ray and I would not have developed this amazing process that has changed so many lives and saved some like mine. For that, words are completely inadequate. I am grateful to her family and friends, who embraced me when I attended Elise's memorial. Their commitment to carrying on the spirit and the work is inspiring, and I hope to continue this movement to see and create a positive and peaceful world.

I want to acknowledge our Genysys Leadership Team of Laurie Reinhart, Neal Welland, Bill Larson, and Ilene Bezjian, who have supported this project and the business. I am also grateful to our current Genysys consultants who have embraced the power of using Strategic Futuring in their own lives and their work with others (Andrea Nunez, Art Gray, Charles Singleton, Dean Wilson, Grace Barnes, Ian Grimbaldeston, Jann Freed, Jay Derrico, Kirk Wells, Laurel Joakimides, and Ralph Plumb).

Thank you, Ilene Bezjian, for pushing to get this book done—even writing a version and following through on your promise that when it is done, you are ready to get it out in the world! I am also grateful to you, Vic Bezjian, for being a great advocate of Strategic Futuring and a model of futuring.

I want to thank the other Genysys Board members: Guy Adams, Joe Johnson, and Blake Rood, who have supported the need to finish this book as a key part of building the business.

I am grateful to Eileen Hulme, who invited me to do a Strategic Futuring Workshop with her students. She is a part of my vision, as I have modeled who I desire to be as a speaker and entrepreneur after her. Thank you for being you. I know we will finally work together some day.

I am grateful to Kathy Rose for being one of my strongest advocates, as she took on writing this book and telling her story. Your encouragement has been priceless. This project may very well have died without your voice.

I am grateful to Karen Brightly, Kristie Haskell, Blanca Siebels, and Julie Wood for caring enough about Strategic Futuring to invest time and energy in developing it further so it can now get into the hands of many more people!

Thank you to Jennifer Moore for taking Ray through his own Strategic Futuring process, for being willing to engage with me as my supervisor in out-of-the-box thinking in my early days with Genysys, and for modeling authenticity.

I am grateful to my friend and colleague, Ray's "brother," John Perry, for sharing his story so freely and allowing our team to utilize his assessment to assist our clients—who find themselves in places similar to his mid-career crisis. I am thankful that he chose his life instead of just a paycheck—and that he continues to do so.

Thank you, Debbie Tonguis, for being the first to go along with Ray's experiment with his graduate students back in 1985. I continue to be impressed by how seriously you have taken your vision, and how you have shared it with me freely, and also shared the Strategic Futuring process with your students so they might also have a vision and a pathway to a positive future. I look forward to part two of your vision, now that you are living your thirty-year vision, and the role that Genysys might play in your next act. Good days are ahead.

Thank you, Eileen, for your bravery in seeking me out and then entrusting me to take you through Strategic Futuring. Our friendship has been incredibly meaningful and affirming. I look forward to ways we will continue to support each other's visions to their full realization.

Thank you to Paul Angone for being Ray's last student and carving a path for yourself that has inspired many to do the same. Thank you for sharing your story and allowing me to spread the word with you. I look forward to seeing how your vision unfolds and ways we might collaborate to help millennials.

Along with Mary-Ellen, I want to thank Kathleen Brown for sharing her story for this book. It is inspiring to see the tangible results of your vision, Kathleen, in the form of the restaurant you started with your brother. I know it will experience great success and I look forward to visiting you in France, when you start your vineyard and when the other part of your vision will come to fruition, literally.

Thank you, Wayne Herron, for openly offering your story and for your enthusiasm in sharing your story with the Genysys group in different settings—and opening doors for more people to experience Strategic Futuring.

Thank you, Lucy Gonzalez, for daring to go through Strategic Futuring and for continuing to take the risks necessary to see your vision realized.

Thank you, Chad Johnson, for asking me to help you in your company in 2006. Without the positive experience of seeing you step into your God-given leadership, I would not have pursued the work I am doing today. You inspired me, and I will continue to be grateful for your humility in reaching out to a young business student and articulating, at the end, the value I brought to you and your company.

I am grateful for Marianne Emma Jeff, and the amazing entrepreneurs at the Women's Business Momentum Center, for supporting me as I wrote this book and continued to build the business. You are an inspiration to me as a female business owner. Thank you to Hazel Ortega, Joanna Vargas, Erica Orosco Cruz, Sarah Greer, Nicola Borland, Brenda Smith, Michelle Summers Colon, Patty Lafond, Jacklyn Green, Colleen McInerney, May Paolin, Liza Rodriguez, Carmen Hall, Mu Larson, Charlyn d'Anconia, Brandye Wilson-Manigat, Carmen Torres, Veronica Corona, Kim Quick, Rochelle James, Vanessa Hidalgo, Lisa Duncan, and Mari Fong for your encouragement and your example of being amazing business divas.

Thank you to Jessica Colp, my Strategic Partner, for your commitment to your own vision and for helping me find a way to do partnering in a way that really works and is fun!

Thank you, Julia Satterlee—you are a kindred spirit and great source of inspiration and support because of the way you have dared to stand in your own authenticity and not stay small.

Thank you to my group in Boston, the MassBay (Massachusetts Bay Community College) Organizational Development Learning Group (MBODLG), for your inspiration in the early days of my vision—Clarissa Sawyer, Jim Murphy, Carol Sharicz, and Julia Geisman for being my first OD mentors and being willing to help me "toughen up." And thanks to Jonathan Mozenter, Kristine Dunn Buonopane, Claudia Lach, Jennifer Rose, Ernest Byers, Toby Elwin, and the late Charley Matera (I still think fondly of all of our car rides together to MBODLG team meetings and Charley's investment in me in the early days).

Thank you to Robert Quinn, author of *Deep Change: Discovering the Leader Within*,[1] one of the foundational books all of our consultants read because it speaks to the primary assumption every person faces—slow death or deep change. I am a fan of your work, including *Building the Bridge as You Walk on It: A Guide for Leading Change*,[2] *Lift: The Fundamental State of Leadership*,[3] and *Letters to Garrett: Stories of Change, Power and Possibility*.[4]

Thank you, David Whyte. Yours was the first book Ray had me read and that spoke so powerfully to the pain I was experiencing on the job. Thank you for writing *The Heart Aroused: Poetry and Preservation of the Soul in Corporate America*.[5]

Thank you to Seth Godin for the powerful insights you provided in your book Tribes. This profoundly changed my view of how I wanted to approach engaging people in my world.[6]

I wish to thank Oprah for inspiring my first vision of being myself, by daring to live an authentic life. You will always be an inspiration to me.

ABOUT THE AUTHOR

PRISCILLA ROSE

Priscilla Rose is an experienced manager. Through a consulting partnership to assist a family-owned business, she first connected with Ray Rood of the Genysys Group and was able to successfully introduce the Genysys transformational change model to support a shift in the organization that produced significant bottom-line results. She continues to work with individuals and organizations to assist them in culture change. As CEO of The Genysys Group, Priscilla focuses the rest of her time on leading Genysys in its own transformation to become a thought leader and change agent by bringing the Genysys products and services to the many individuals and organizations that need support in creating the futures they truly desire. She is excited to collaborate with her Genysys colleagues to write this book about those who have *dared* to take the leap and choose their futures by going through the signature process, Strategic Futuring!

ABOUT GENYSYS GROUP

The Genysys Group is a change facilitation firm working with individuals and organizations to help them overcome obstacles and translate their dreams into reality. We live, lead, and work with a deep understanding of human development and change management. Our distinction is the use of *vision* as a source of the clarity and energy needed for any significant change.

FOREWORD AND EPILOGUE BY RAY ROOD

Raymond Rood is Founder and Senior Consultant of The Genysys Group, a firm offering organizational development / transformational support to for-profit and not-for-profit organizations and public agencies worldwide that are seeking to initiate, sustain, and/or safeguard long-term change. His consulting and teaching have taken him to all continents and enabled him to work in over thirty countries.

Ray is an experienced executive, consultant, program designer, developer, facilitator, presenter, and educator. His experience ranges from consulting with Fortune 500 companies to start-up organizations, focusing on the areas of change management, executive coaching, and board development. He served as the founding Dean of the International Forum for Child Welfare's Executive Institute on Leadership and Organizational Development, designed for child welfare executives worldwide.

Ray is the founder of graduate degree programs in Student Development Education and Human Resource Leadership at Azusa Pacific University, where he has been involved for more than forty years. For over ten years, he served as a member of the Azusa Pacific University Board of Trustees, including four years as vice chairman.

Ray defines his work as helping organizations and individuals to realize great dreams.

NOTES

FOREWORD

1. This story is adapted from a Russian fairy tale called *The Firebird, the Horse of Power, and the Princess Vasilissa*, captured by British author Arthur Ransome in his book *Old Peter's Russian Tales* (Thomas Nelson, 1916; Jonathan Cape, 1984; Jane Nissen Books, 2003).

INTRODUCTION

1. Behavioral psychologist Albert Ellis coined the phrase "tyranny of the 'shoulds'" in his book *Reason and Emotion in Psychotherapy* (revised and updated, Secaucus, NJ: Carol Publishing Group, 1994).

2. Michel Foucault, *Discipline and Punish: The Birth of the Prison* (New York: Random House, 1975).

CHAPTER 2

1. Robert Quinn, *Deep Change: Discovering the Leader Within* (Jossey-Bass, 1996).

2. Erik H. Erikson, *Childhood and Society* (W. W. Norton and Company, Inc., 1950).

3. Donald Clifton and Marcus Buckingham, *Now, Discover Your Strengths: How to Develop Your Talents and Those of the People You Manage* (Simon and Schuster, 2006).

CHAPTER 4

1. a). Elise Boulding, *Building a Global Civic Culture: Education for an Interdependent World* (Peace and Conflict Resolution, Syracuse University Press, 2000); b) Elise Boulding, *Cultures of Peace: The Hidden Side of History* (Syracuse Studies on Peace and Conflict Resolution; Syracuse University Press, 2000).

2. Paulo Coelho, *The Alchemist* (Harper One, 2014).

CHAPTER 6

1. Gary Keller and Jay Papasan, *The ONE Thing: The Surprisingly Simple Truth Behind Extraordinary Results* (Bard Press, 2013).

2. Robert Quinn, *Building the Bridge as You Walk on It: A Guide for Leading Change* (Jossey-Bass, 2004).

CHAPTER 8

1. Robert Quinn, *Deep Change: Discovering the Leader Within* (Jossey-Bass, 1996).

EPILOGUE

1. Robert Frost, *The Road Not Taken* (Mountain Interval, Henry Colt and Company, 1916).

ACKNOWLEDGMENTS

1. Robert Quinn, *Deep Change: Discovering the Leader Within* (Jossey-Bass, 1996).

2. Robert Quinn, *Building the Bridge as You Walk on It: A Guide for Leading Change* (Jossey-Bass, 2004).

3. Ryan W. Quinn and Robert E. Quinn, *Lift: The Fundamental State of Leadership* (2nd edition, Berrett-Koehler Publishers, 2015).

4. Robert E. Quinn and Garrett T. Quinn, *Letters to Garrett: Stories of Change, Power and Possibility* (Jossey-Bass, 2002).

5. David Whyte, *The Heart Aroused: Poetry and Preservation of the Soul in Corporate America* (Crown Business, 1996).

6. Seth Godin, *Tribes: We Need You to Lead Us* (Portfolio, 2008).

JOIN THE TRIBE OF PEOPLE WHO HAVE PICKED UP THE GOLDEN FEATHER TO BECOME A STRATEGIC FUTURIST

Join our email list to receive regular updates—go to YourDaringFuture.com

Join the Facebook Strategic Futurists Private Group

- Receive regular notes of inspiration or resources to assist you on your journey
- Share your experiences with the tribe
  - Celebrate the small and large "wins"!
  - Share challenges and questions for feedback from others who have had a similar challenge
- Be in the know about opportunities to connect with your tribe
  - Group coaching
  - Strategic Partnering

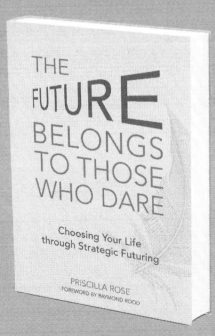

Spread the word. You have picked up this Golden Feather. Gift another Golden Feather to a friend who may desire a shift in their life!

Made in the USA
San Bernardino, CA
06 May 2017